The Church on the Brink

THE CHURCH ON THE BRINK

Paul B. Smith

TYNDALE HOUSE PUBLISHERS, INC.

WHEATON, ILLINOIS

All Scripture quotations, except where otherwise indicated, are taken
from the King James Version.
Library of Congress Catalog Card Number 77-080733. ISBN 0-8423-0278-6,
paper. Copyright © 1977 by Paul B. Smith. All rights reserved. First printing,
November 1977. Printed in the United States of America.

CONTENTS

Foreword 7
Preface 9

One The Need of the Church: Revival 13
1 Prologue to Revival 15
2 When Revival Is Necessary 19
3 How Revival Happens 35
4 What Revival Does 48

Two The Challenge of the Church: Gifts of the Spirit 75
5 Gifts of the Spirit—Used or Abused? 77
6 What Does the Bible Say about Tongues? 96
7 First Corinthians Twelve 104
8 First Corinthians Fourteen 112
9 Is Tongues the Evidence of the Infilling
   of the Spirit? 124

Three The Solution of the Church: Love 135
10 From Tongues to Love 137
11 The Derivation of Love 139
12 The Dynamic of Love 144
13 The Definition of Love 150
14 The Duration of Love 179

Four The Message of the Church: The Gospel 183
15 From Secondary Messages to the Gospel 185
16 The Apostle and His Religion 189
17 The Apostle and His Righteousness 197
18 The Apostle and His Race 207
19 The Apostle and His Road 216

Epilogue 223

FOREWORD

It gives me great pleasure to write a foreword to
The Church on the Brink by my longtime friend and
pastor, Dr. Paul B. Smith, senior minister of The
Peoples Church in Toronto. Being an elder of
The Peoples Church, I have personally heard much of
this material given and have shared the impact
which it registered, not only on my own life, but on
the thousands of others who were present when it
was preached.

I first met and heard Paul B. Smith a quarter of a
century ago. He was then an evangelist crusading
to the masses in Britain. I have since encountered
innumerable of those who were blessed by his crusades
in Southern Africa, New Zealand, Australia, Sweden,
the Caribbean, and throughout North America.

Not only is he an evangelist, pastor, and conference
preacher, but he is also known around the world
as a foremost evangelical author, apologist,
administrator, missionary statesman, and Christian
educator. As pastor of The Peoples Church, he is
successor to his father, Dr. Oswald J. Smith. In the last
two decades that congregation has reached out to
the world through an annual world missions budget of
well over a million dollars, supporting in part
more than 400 missionaries.

Committed unequivocably to biblical inerrancy, the
Lordship of Christ, and the Spirit-filled life, Paul
Smith possesses a rare gift for friendship. In those
whom he touches he inspires great allegiance and
affection. Yet he is a humble man, as genuinely
anxious to know Christ better as he is to make him
better known. And just here is perhaps the key to his
worldwide ministry. People who see and hear Paul B.

Smith, close up or far away, cannot fail to see that
here is a man from God whose hallmark is his
monumental modesty; whose sympathy and empathy
with human need springs from his intimate walk with
God.

   As I read through the pages of this book, I could feel
the same spiritual pulsations which I experience
in hearing Paul B. Smith preach. I'm sure that once you
have read *The Church on the Brink,* you will want
to pass it on!

John Wesley White
Associate Evangelist,
Billy Graham Evangelistic Association
Toronto, Canada
January 1977

PREFACE

One of the marks of maturity is tolerance toward others, particularly in areas where there is room for a difference of opinion. In the arena of Christian truth we must be dogmatic where the Bible is dogmatic. This would certainly cover all of the basic doctrines, the fundamentals, which have always formed the core of the creeds of every major Christian denomination. Much of our disagreement with other Christians has been in regards to those peripheral problems that for sovereign reasons God does not choose to clarify for us completely.

Young people and young organizations are sometimes dogmatic where the Scriptures are not dogmatic, and in the exuberance and sophomoric spirit of the young they are often very explosive about their own opinions, opinions that may not have had enough exposure to reality to be viable.

The subject matter of these pages is not at all new in my ministry. I have been preaching on these topics for more than thirty-five years. However, as I remember some of the books I wrote many years ago, I am amazed at how young I was and how little I knew. I am still overwhelmed at the universe of knowledge of which I still know only a small amount, even about those tiny planets that orbit around my own finite world of religious matters.

I don't think that any of my fundamental beliefs have changed, but they have needed to be said in a more gracious manner; and where there is room within the Scriptures for a variety of interpretations, I have tried to be less opinionated. I hope this means that by the grace of God I have matured to some degree, and I pray that some of my devout "friends" will not suggest that my faith has deteriorated.

A good example of this kind of maturity can be seen in the *New Scofield Reference Bible*. While not changing in any marked degree the intention of the original editors, the new edition has left some breathing room for those who do not accept all of the structure of the Scofield approach to Bible study— which, of course, is a good outline or method developed by a good man, but is not part of the inspired Word. In the notes explaining that difficult verse in Second Thessalonians (2:7), the old edition says, "This Person can be *no other than* the Holy Spirit in the church" (italics mine). The new edition has grown up to the extent that it says, "There are various views as to the identity of the restraining influence . . . It seems evident that it is the Holy Spirit" (pp. 1272, 1295).

In this way the new edition has said exactly the same thing, but has left room for a difference of interpretation in a matter that all honest Bible students know is not completely clarified within the Scriptures.

I have also taken the liberty of putting down in black and white what most Christian leaders discuss eventually almost every time they get together—that is, the charismatic movement. This is not intended to be a vindication of those of us who are not charismatic, nor a criticism of those who are. My contacts around the world have proved adequately to me that there are very godly and extremely effective people on both sides of this particular fence—and maybe even a few that are still sitting on it.

My use of the word "charismatic" is in the modern sense—we should all be aware of the fact that this has become a sort of umbrella expression that describes a group of people who have chosen to emphasize a certain area of Christian truth in a particular manner. I do not use the word purely in its biblical form, which is an anglicized rendition of a Greek word meaning "grace-gifts." In the sense of believing in the gifts of the Holy Spirit, every Christian must be charismatic because there is no escaping the person, work, gifts, and fruit of the Holy Spirit as a part of the teaching of the Bible.

It is my hope that even in this area that is very controversial at the present time, I have approached it graciously and with at least some degree of Christian maturity. If you choose to disagree with me, "join the club," as long as you remain within the limits of biblical teaching and have developed your opinions from a foundation of sound exegesis that would be acceptable to any honest scholar who starts from the historic position of the church through the centuries—that the Bible is completely infallible in all areas.

P. B. S.
Toronto, Canada
September 1976

PART ONE
The Need of the Church: Revival

CHAPTER ONE
PROLOGUE
TO REVIVAL

God may not choose to do things tomorrow in exactly the same way he did them yesterday. The Bible stresses the fact that God does not change, but it is quite obvious that he does not deal with all of us in the same manner.

Most of us have difficulty in accepting this. Sometimes we talk as if everyone should go through the same kind of an emotional experience when they are converted and that we should also have the same experience when the Holy Spirit takes control of our lives. This is probably a result of hearing a number of personal testimonies about these experiences. Testimonies may be one of the best means of communicating the gospel, but we need to be careful to separate a person's commitment to Christ or his filling of the Spirit from the events that took place in his life before, during, and after these experiences. As a matter of fact, it is doubtful whether any two people have had experiences that are identical in every respect.

I am going to discuss revival in some detail in the chapters that follow, and I hope that I will manage to avoid the error of assuming that we can expect an exact repetition of former revivals. Certain basic patterns may always be the same, but many of the stories we read about those days have more to do with the culture of the times, the theological positions of the people, the size of the communities, and the general God-consciousness that was usually predominant even among nonchurchgoers, agnostics, and professed atheists.

Some of the rather dramatic incidents and results of the "old" revivals may never be repeated. Indeed, some of these may now be quite impossible. It is unlikely that we will ever see an entire modern community turn to God—except perhaps in some quite small and thinly populated places. The older preachers such as Wesley, Whitefield, Finney, Moody, Booth, and even the more recent Billy Sunday and Gypsy Smith, preached in a world in which the grass-roots public believed the Bible even though many of them had not made a personal commitment to Christ. Indeed, the earlier list had the happy situation of ministry in churches whose colleges and seminaries had not crossed over the great divide into the chaos of a weak view of inspiration.

To my knowledge there is no such community in the world today, apart from a few primitive groups that haven't been Christians long enough to have been weakened by those who want to bear the label of Christianity despite the fact that they have long since discarded the Book.

In addition to the frustration of preaching about the Bible in areas that do not believe the Bible, we live in a society that is highly urban and very much overpopulated. Despite the miracle of mass media, it is very difficult to get any message of any kind to everybody in a modern, densely populated city. The revivalists in the "olden days" worked in relatively small towns and cities among people who for the most part already believed the Bible.

One of the most exciting side effects of former revivals was the social change that often took place. Saloons closed down, crime diminished, and in Wales it is said that the donkeys that worked in the mines had to learn a new language because their drivers had suddenly stopped cursing.

Nothing is more thrilling than to read these stories, but nothing is more dangerous than to direct our prayers for revival in such a way that we begin to expect these same things to take place again in our times. We must always remember that these social changes were the by-products of particular revivals and will perhaps never happen in the same way again. Revival concerns the relationship of an individual with his God and the ramifications of that relationship in his own life. Revival does not in itself involve the closing of a bar or a brothel that is run by an unbeliever who may not even be aware that people are being revived.

We should also remember that a revival may not be transported from one place to another simply by transporting some of the key figures that God used in that revival. The human instrument of the revival in the Hebrides has ministered in Toronto. His messages were most effective and deeply spiritual, but nothing unusual occurred. Some of the leaders who had been involved in the revival in Saskatoon, Saskatchewan, visited Toronto churches, and although they went through the same motions nothing much happened.

It would be an easy out to blame it on the Christians of Toronto, or perhaps the more biblical answer would have to be that God is sovereign and he alone determines when and where there will be a widespread movement of the Holy Spirit that future generations will look back on and call "revival."

This leads us to the burden of the next few chapters; that is, revival in the life of an individual Christian, in a single church, or community. Meetings may not last all night, the dirty linen of the church may not be aired before the general public, bars and brothels may continue to flourish, and agnosticism may remain untouched, but we can still see revival—real revival, biblical revival, revival that may only affect a few lives directly but through them in some way wraps its arms around a lost world.

CHAPTER TWO
WHEN REVIVAL
IS NECESSARY

The seven churches in Asia mentioned in the first chapters of the book of Revelation are accused by Jesus of at least five things, all showing the need of revival.

First, the church at Ephesus, in chapter two, verse four: " . . . thou hast left thy first love."

Second and third, the church in Pergamos, in chapter two, verses fourteen and fifteen: " . . . thou hast there them that hold the doctrine of Balaam . . . So hast thou also them that hold the doctrine of the Nicolaitans."

Fourth, the church in Sardis, in chapter three, verse one: " . . . thou hast a name that thou livest, and art dead."

Finally, Laodicea, in chapter three, verses fifteen and sixteen: " . . . thou art neither cold nor hot."

Whatever predictive significance the message of Christ to these churches of Asia may have had, there is no doubt that his message did have an immediate application to seven actually existing bodies of Christian people. Although these chapters of the Revelation very likely refer in part to the spiritual progress of the Christian church from her inception to the Second Advent of her Lord, one can scarcely read these verses without realizing that Jesus was condemning particular churches for spiritual deficiencies that demanded their immediate attention.

The churches in question were in many respects quite commendable, and the Lord does not hesitate to point out these good qualities; but, with the possible exception of the church of Philadelphia, each of them lacked something that robbed it of its power and influence. Even the Philadelphian church is represented as having only a "little strength." It does no violence, then, to the context to conclude that the seven churches of Asia in John's day needed revival.

"THOU HAST LEFT THY FIRST LOVE"

In many instances throughout the Bible, the love of a man for his Lord is expressed in terms of the love of a bride for her husband. Likewise, the love of God for man is quite often compared to the love of a man for his wife. Thus, human relationships can illustrate the two-way love that flows between God and man.

There are three outstanding characteristics of the "first love" of one person for another in the human realm—enthusiasm, fellowship, and service—and they are a commentary of what our love for God should be like.

Enthusiasm. Listen to the girl who is in love for the first time. The conversation of others is about things in general, but she cannot refrain from speaking continually, to anyone who will listen, about the man of her choice and the object of her love. Let some slightly detrimental remark be made about him, and immediately she takes the floor to defend him and to sing his praises. A girl friend may casually compare him with others, but for her there is no comparison. She cannot say too much about him. No commendation is too great. Nothing but superlatives will suffice in her expression of her "first love."

There is little that is stronger than the intense

enthusiasm of newly born love. There are few
calamities so devastating to human love as the loss of
that early enthusiasm.

Many Christians look back on the excitement they
used to have with a tinge of remorse. Now they
serve Christ grudgingly. They remember the early days
of Christian experience with something of regret
as they recall the enthusiasm that has long since
waned and almost disappeared. There was a day when
it seemed that "a thousand tongues" would have
been far too few to sing their "great Redeemer's praise,"
but now they must confess that their one tongue has
been silent about the Savior for many weeks. They used
to look for the openings that would enable them to
give their testimony, but today they deliberately
close the door on the most obvious opportunities.

They no longer have that "first love."

Fellowship. The person in love longs to be with the
one he loves.

A man will take immediate advantage of the
slightest opportunity to be with his girl friend. He will
break appointments, leave his work undone, go
without a meal, or do almost anything, if only he can
satisfy the cry of his heart to be near her.

What a boon to human love is this longing to be
together! How barren human love becomes when
lovers are content to be apart!

Strong is the desire of the young Christian to be near
the divine object of his love. Wherever the presence
of the Lord is felt, that is where he longs to be.
As he pores over his Bible and then opens up his heart
to God in prayer, he is conscious of the nearness
of his Savior, and spends much time in devotional
fellowship with him. The believer knows that "where

two or three are gathered together" in Jesus' name
he will be in their midst, and he makes it a point to be
in prayer meetings, Bible classes, evangelistic
campaigns, anywhere that his Christ is exalted and he
can be more conscious of his nearness.

What a tragedy that many of us must admit that we
no longer crave the presence of our Lord. There is a
longing to be at the club or lodge, there is a desire to be
at sports play-offs, there is an urge to be in society—to
listen to fine music, read the latest books, watch the
most popular TV programs, spend quiet evenings at
home with the family—but there is a dreadful absence
of the early desire of our hearts to be in the
presence of Jesus.

We have lost the longing to be near which
characterized our "first love."

Desire to Serve. Probably the greatest single
indication of strong human love, and its most binding
characteristic, is the desire to serve that is always
manifest in its early stages.

Is there any service that requires too much effort
on the part of the lover for his beloved? On the
contrary, it would seem that the greater the effort, the
more trying the sacrifice, the more painstaking
the work, the greater the satisfaction.

As the anthology of great human love is scanned,
page after page, it declares the immeasurable extent to
which some have gone to demonstrate their love.

Is there any greater desire in the heart of the young
Christian than to serve the Lord Jesus Christ? Is any
service too great for the Lord? If only we could rise
from the altar and go directly to the martyr's stake,
how happy we would be. "Jesus has done so much for
me; what can I do for him? He has given all for me; let

me begin now to exhaust myself in service for him."

The new convert enters upon a Christian life of active sacrificial service.

If only every mature child of God had the same desire to serve that he had early in his love for the Lord! But such is not the case. Many older Christians must confess that the fires of service have burned low. The flow of service that gushed from their lives when first they drank from the Living Water has long since ebbed, and in many cases dried up completely. They carried the torch of sacrificial service for a short time, but before long it fell by the wayside of spiritual lethargy and complacency.

They are active at school, busy with the community chest, diligent for the service club, helpful at home, energetic at the office, untiring in their efforts of patriotism—but dormant in service for God.

They have lost the desire to serve that was one of the dominant characteristics of their "first love."

Jesus saw the personal devotion of his followers as the final test of their discipleship. Before leaving his little group of followers to take his place at the right hand of the Father, he selected Peter from the rest of the men and put to him this final test of loyalty: "Simon, son of Jonas, lovest thou me . . .?" (John 21:15).

With this question Jesus once and for all placed personal love for himself beyond all else. In Ephesus he saw a group of Christians who were doctrinally sound, absolutely faithful, and extremely patient, but he condemned them for their lack of that personal devotion to him that had been so prominent in the early days of their Christian lives.

The Christian who has ever been more intensely enthusiastic about the Lord, experienced a greater longing for his presence, desired more to serve the

Master than today has undoubtedly lost that "first love" and needs revival.

"THE DOCTRINE OF BALAAM"

After their experience with the fiery serpents, the Israelites made a fairly rapid and victorious march through the wilderness toward the Jordan River. Before them stood only one kingdom, the land of the Moabites, which separated them from their destination, the land of Canaan. Balak, the king, had seen with some fear this uninterrupted march through the other kingdoms. Apparently he sensed the fact that the children of Israel had on their side some mysterious force which carried them through any and all opposition. Unless he could undermine this unseen power, his armies would be defeated in battle as had the others against whom the Israelites had fought. In accordance with this view, he sent for the prophet Balaam and paid him to put a curse on the armies of Israel.

The book of Numbers tells the story of Balaam's futile attempts to curse Israel and of Balak's growing fear. Each time that the unworthy prophet opened his mouth, the Lord forced him to bless the people rather than curse them.

Finally, Balaam changed his course of action. Instead of trying to curse the people, he began to spread the false doctrine that now, contrary to the explicit command of the Lord, they should feel free to mingle with the Moabites, marry the Moabite women, and take part in the Moabites' heathen religion. Many of the people followed Balaam's advice, and the result was a plague that killed 24,000 of them, halted the immediate progress of their armies, and robbed them, temporarily at least, of their vast power (Numbers 22—25 and 31:16).

Israel was successful as long as the people maintained a wall of separation between themselves and the heathen tribes around them. The moment this barrier was removed, they lost their power. The church of Pergamos had a good witness before the world as long as there remained a clear-cut mark of distinction between the Christians and the heathen tribes around them. When they let down the bars of separation by following the doctrine of Balaam and mingling with the ungodly peoples on every side of them, they lost their power and their influence. The Pergamos Christians needed revival because they had failed to separate themselves from the evil practices and degrading influences of the world in which they lived.

If Jesus Christ were to speak directly to the modern church as he did through John to the church of Pergamos, there is no doubt but that he would condemn some of us as in need of revival because of our lack of separation. A large percentage of Christians today could not deny such an accusation. It takes no special revelation to point out the fact that the twentieth-century church in many areas seems to have lost its power with God and with men, but how slow most of us are to admit that this loss of power and influence is due so often to lack of separation from the world. It was only while the Israelites could claim to be a "peculiar people" that God demonstrated his power in their lives, and it is only as we are able to claim the same distinction that God is able to use us to manifest his power to the world.

Thousands of God's children find themselves impotent today for this very reason. Church after church has lost its testimony because there is no longer any distinction between its members and the men and women of the world. Instead of raising the standards, and thus regaining their power from God, the policy of many churches has been to lower standards to increase membership. In the early church anything that was in any way tainted with the world was considered wrong, but today sin has been white-washed to make easy access into the church. The apostolic Christian was anxious to get as far away from the world and the things of the world as possible. The modern Christian seems to be most concerned about how far into the world one can go and still be safe. Such a Christian differs only in name from the people of the world and has little, if anything, to offer unbelievers. How can such a testimony be effective?

Hundreds upon hundreds of worldly people are searching for something they do not possess. We have in Christ the end of that search—a transformed life in which "old things have passed away and all things have become new," a life that is different in every respect from that of the world, a life that is distinct, a life that is peculiar, a life that is wholly separated—not only *from* the world, but *to* Jesus Christ. The only hope that we have of influencing people is in a personal demonstration of the fact that we have found in the Son of God what the people of the world are hungry to have. When we lose the marks that distinguish us from the worldly crowd, we lose our testimony and need revival.

"THE DOCTRINE OF THE NICOLAITANS"

It is true that there are different gifts within the church of Jesus Christ—"some, apostles; and some, prophets; and some, evangelists; and some, pastors and teachers"—but the Word of God gives no ground for spiritual superiority among Christians. The church has various gifts, but it is one body in Christ.

The "doctrine of the Nicolaitans" set up in the church a spiritual hierarchy by drawing a distinct line of demarcation between the laity and the clergy. When this philosophy seeped into the otherwise united body of Christ, it left the door wide open for the development of spiritual pride. Jesus accuses the Pergamos church of this doctrine, and he emphasizes the fact that it is a thing he "hates."

This paradox of phraseology, *spiritual* pride, has always been one of the greatest barriers to the development of spiritual power both in Christian churches and in the lives of individual Christian people. God cannot use the believer who has begun to look down on others. There is no greater hindrance to revival than people who feel that they have attained spiritually and now stand head and shoulders above others. The person who thinks himself superior in the things of the Spirit is a powerless Christian. The Christian who is proud is not spiritual, and the Christian who is spiritual is not proud.

If any Christian ever had the right to feel that he was superior to others, it was the Apostle Paul. He had done so much in his service for the Lord that he might well have looked back upon his life toward the end and considered himself to have advanced far beyond the spirituality of others, if not to have almost attained perfection. What a testimony he had! There is no false modesty about the apostle. He admitted many times that he had gained much ground for God, and on several occasions he stopped to list his experiences and achievements—shipwrecked, beaten with stripes, imprisoned, stoned, ridiculed, driven out of cities, etc. He was the founder of many of the early Christian churches. He was the writer, under God, of roughly half of the New Testament. Paul, of all Christians, had more reason to boast than others.

What is his testimony? Does he consider himself to have arrived spiritually? Does he think that he has gone as far as he can go? Listen to his own words after years of service:

"Not as though I had already attained, either were already perfect: but I follow after, if that I may apprehend that for which also I am apprehended of Jesus Christ. Brethren, I count not myself to have apprehended: but this one thing I do, forgetting those things which are behind, and reaching forth unto those things which are before, I press toward the mark for the prize of the high calling of God in Christ Jesus" (Philippians 3:12-14).

Paul had just finished listing the things he could brag about, and then he made this statement, "forgetting those things which are behind." The victories of the past, the blessings of the past, the sacrifice, the ridicule, the persecution, the hardship, and the numerous other things about which he might glory—all were put, as it were, behind his back, and he pledged himself to begin at this point and "press toward the mark," as if he were still only at the starting line spiritually.

This is the testimony of a man whose spirituality makes the greatest attainments of others fade into insignificance. No matter how far we have climbed up the spiritual ladder, alongside the life and sacrifice of the Apostle Paul we are probably still tottering on the first rung. Thank God if we have gained some ground spiritually, but let us beware lest in looking

down on our weaker friends we take our eyes off our
Lord. "Let him that thinketh he standeth take heed
lest he fall" (1 Corinthians 10:12).

The Christians of Pergamos were faithful in the
midst of persecution, but Jesus rebuked them for their
spiritual pride. When any individual child of God or
Christian group develops the same weakness, revival
is necessary, because the Lord hates spiritual pride and
will not manifest his power in the midst of it.

"A NAME—AND ART DEAD"

The church of Sardis needed revival because her
reputation was greater than her life—"Thou hast a
name that thou livest, and art dead." Here was a
church whose profession of Christianity was greater
than her possession. No doubt the fame of this church
had been spread abroad. If it were existing today,
it would probably be reckoned among the more
important evangelical centers. It was a church that had
apparently done a great work for Christ in its early
days. It had among its members some Christians who
had been known for their fervor and incessant witness
during past days of spiritual awakening. The fame
had been maintained throughout the years, but the
spiritual life of the people had declined; and when
the Lord sends this message to the church through the
pen of John, he gives a true picture of it—famous,
but dead.

How many churches and temples throughout the
Christian world today might well give heed to the
message of Christ to this church of the first century.
How many of us love to talk of "the good old days"
—days of revival, of soul-winning, of crowds that
thronged to hear the gospel, of the movement of the

Spirit of God, of enthusiasm, zeal, fervor, and, in short, all the other earmarks of a work that is alive and on fire for the Lord.

But look at many of the same churches now. They still have the reputation. Preachers still think it's a privilege to stand in their pulpits. Visitors to the city have not seen everything until they have been to a service. Their fame has gone to and fro throughout the vast Christian world; but, alas, if the truth were known, they are dead. There they stand, a monument to another age when God worked through them, but just as devoid of real spiritual life as a wax statue. They have the form, but they have no vitality.

There is only one reason for this dearth of life in so many of our churches today. The individual Christians in such churches are on a small scale what the whole church is on a larger scale. It is the individuals that make the church, and where the church has no vitality, we may safely conclude that the members have none. Their name is Ichabod.

When our profession becomes greater than our possession, when the shell becomes more important than the kernel, when the shadow of spiritual power takes the place of the actual substance, or when our church has a name that it lives but in reality is dead, we need revival.

It has always been easy to fool the world. The average person is quite gullible. Most anybody can convince other people that he is fairly spiritual, but God sees the heart. God looks beyond the mere profession. He is not concerned about the shell. He does not notice the shadow. He probes beneath the veneer of nominalism and superficiality. People only know what we profess to be, but God knows what we actually are.

The Christian or the church whose life does not support in every detail the testimony that is given to the world needs revival.

"NEITHER COLD NOR HOT"

In the prophetic interpretation of this passage of Scripture, the Laodicean church would typify the modern liberal church. It was neither cold nor hot, but lukewarm. What a true picture of modernism this is! Here was a church that was not violently opposed to anything, nor was it overwhelmingly in favor of anything. It was not fervent in its love for the Lord, but it did not go so far as to deny him blatantly. It did not battle to uphold the faith, because it had no definite faith for which it wished to contend.

Many people have a false idea of what a "modernist" really is. The name is usually taken to signify a person who is defiantly opposed to the fundamental teachings of the Word of God. A modernist is thought to be one who denies all the basic elements of gospel truth. That particular brand of modernism has long since been outmoded; the anti-blood, anti-virgin birth, anti-sin, anti-hell, anti-soul type of modernism has for quite some time been a thing of the past. The modernists of today do not deny anything, but are not convicted about anything either. They are liberal in the true sense of the world. The other person's belief is just as good as theirs, and theirs is every bit as good as anyone else's. Lack of conviction is the essential weakness of most modern teachers, preachers, and theologians. Really, a better word for today's liberal is "agnostic." He just doesn't know and I'm not at all sure he's trying to find out.

This was the accusation made against the Laodicean

Christians. They were in no wise defiant sinners,
nor were they by any means ardent saints. They were
neutral—an impossibility actually. The only kind of
Christians who can make any impact upon the world
with their message are those who are convinced that
they are proclaiming the only truth. Christians who
have lost their conviction in regard to the inspiration
and teaching of the Word of God are in need of revival.
People cannot convince others unless they are
convinced themselves. That is why the modern church
has lost out with the people of the world. It has
lost its note of assurance. The world is in a turmoil of
agnosticism. God help the Christian who has nothing
more to offer the world than what it already has in
abundance! The world will listen to the person who
can say, "I know," but it has no time for the
lukewarm, apathetic individual who is unsure.

Inspiration. We need to be convicted, first, about the
inspiration of the Bible. If we cannot say that we
are absolutely certain that the Bible is the infallible
Word of God, completely true and reliable in all
matters, we might just as well have done with it. What
value is any sacred book when mere people become
the criterion of its authenticity? Such a Bible is fit
only to be shelved with all the other relics of an era
past and gone. Christians who have no real conviction
about the inspiration of the Bible need either to
drop the name "Christian" or begin to pray for revival
in their own lives—despite the fact that they may
still be called evangelicals.

Doctrines. The person who is of any value to the
Lord should have a deep conviction about the major
doctrines of the Bible and should be able to proclaim

those truths without reservation. The atonement
of Christ, his deity, the sin of man, and God's plan
of reconciliation are among those essential truths
about which the child of God should have definite
convictions. Liberals can only say, "We think,"
and thus their influence over others is nil. The world
will pay attention to the person who can say
with confidence, "This is the way; walk ye in it."
Agnosticism is the keynote of the age; the church
could win a great victory for God if it could rise up as
one and say, "We know whereof we speak." Christians
who have lost their conviction about the doctrines
of the faith need revival.

Ethics. Certainly, we cannot command very much
respect if we have no conviction about the ethics of
the Bible. It seems to be the custom of the modern
church to let everyone give their own interpretation of
Christian ethics. There is very little of that convincing
preaching today that cries out in the very face of
sin, "Thus saith the Lord!" Modern Christians seem to
have forgotten that the Lord said anything at all,
and they proceed to give their own interpretation of
sin. They decide what they feel to be right and wrong
and never stop to realize that nobody cares what
they think. The world wants to know what God has to
say, and the person who cannot give a convincing
answer is a poor specimen of Christianity indeed.

The Word of God has something very definite to say
about such things as murder, anger, hatred, theft,
divorce, immorality, envy, jealousy, and a host of other
things. The average Christian worries and exhorts
and scolds about four or five trivial evils that are not
even mentioned in the Bible, and at the same time
fails to condemn the sins that are discussed and

condemned from Genesis to Revelation. When the child of God loses conviction about the ethics of biblical religion, revival is necessary.

The Laodicean church was one that Jesus loved, and as a result of this love he spoke very harshly to it. He did not condemn it for its inactivity. Apparently this church was renowned for its "works," but the Lord accused it severely for its lack of conviction. The people had no fiery zeal in their work, nor could they be accused of frigid unbelief. They were simply neutral—"lukewarm"—and thus of no real value to the cause of Christ. Whenever Christians drift down the stream of agnosticism and adopt a lukewarm attitude, lacking the conviction of truth that gives them power in their work for God, they need revival.

Here, then, are five indications of the need for revival in the life of any individual Christian or in the life of any Christian church—loss of love for the Lord, lack of separation from the world, spiritual pride, nominalism, and agnosticism. When any one of these is in evidence, revival is impossible; but when these have been pointed out by the Holy Spirit and are dealt with by the Christian, the way for revival is open.

CHAPTER THREE
HOW REVIVAL HAPPENS

It is quite true that God has promised in his Word
to do a great many things for Christians. But it is also
true that if we are to appropriate the blessing of
God, we must fulfill certain definite conditions which
he has indicated.

God will protect us in heavy traffic, but obviously
he also expects us to watch where we are going.
Physical health is the heritage of Christians in most
cases, but when we slip into a life of intemperance and
live without regard for health we cannot expect the
Lord to do much for us. The Lord has promised to
protect Christians forced into the "midst of their
enemies," but there is no promise of protection for
those who walk deliberately into the path of danger
when they could have avoided it. The Lord gives
journeying mercies to his children as they travel from
one place to another, but it would seem logical
to believe that the guardian angel steps out of our car
when we defy the speed limit. God will send the
sunshine and rain that will bring a good harvest to the
farmer, but can any man expect God to do his plowing
and planting for him?

In almost every phase of life there are certain
obvious conditions that must be fulfilled before
Christians can expect God to bless them.

Revival is no exception to this rule. The one who
sits idly by and waits and longs for revival will
probably never see it. God will revive his people. God
will "forgive their sin, and ... heal their land."

God will manifest his power among them. However, there are certain specific conditions laid down for the blessing of God, and we cannot expect to hear from God until the conditions for revival have been fulfilled.

When God determined the plan of salvation for helpless sinners, he made the way as easy as possible —nothing to do, only believe. But when God set forth the conditions of revival for his own people, he did not make the way easy. The conditions are hard. That is probably why there are so many Christians who still need revival; they do not have the courage to pay the price.

There are four conditions in all, contained in one verse of Scripture that has been used by many for years to set forth the way to revival. The conditions are just the same today as they have always been. When we meet these conditions we will be revived; until we fulfill them we can never be revived. "If my people, which are called by my name, shall *humble* themselves, and *pray*, and *seek* my face, and *turn* from their wicked ways; then will I hear from heaven, and will forgive their sin, and will heal their land" (2 Chronicles 7:14).

"HUMBLE"

It is one thing to be humble before men. It is another thing to be humble before God. In this passage of Scripture God is speaking of the relation of his people with himself, not of their relation with the other peoples around them. A great many Christians seem to have the idea that because they have succeeded in being nothing as far as the world is concerned, they have automatically fulfilled the first condition of revival. Quite often one finds them glorying in the fact that they are nobody in the eyes of the world. Upon closer inspection such people will sometimes be found to be very proud spiritually, and obviously they do not know the first thing about humility before God.

It is quite possible to be humble before people and not be humble at all before God, but it is impossible to be humble before God without at the same time being humble before people. Worldly humility is not a stepping-stone to spiritual humility, but rather it is the by-product of it. It is humility before God that is essential to revival, not humility before people.

Just as salvation is possible only as a result of real humility before God on the part of the sinner, so revival is possible only as a result of continuous humility before God on the part of the saint. Those who are the children of God today can usually remember that there was a time in their lives when they realized that in the eyes of God they were nothing, mere worthless, hell-deserving sinners; and grovelling in the dust of humility before their Maker, they cried out for salvation. People who have never had that experience cannot be Christians, for it is only as they see their own unrighteousness that they plead for the righteousness of Christ to cover them. Sinners come before God saying:

Nothing in my hand I bring,
Simply to Thy cross I cling;
Naked, come to Thee for dress,
Helpless, look to Thee for grace;
Foul, I to the fountain fly,
Wash me, Saviour, or I die.

The moment they do God saves them, and thus humility before God must precede salvation. They are

nothing in themselves, but through the grace of
God they are saved.

Revival becomes necessary when we lose sight of
the grace of God in our Christian experience. No
matter how long Christians live, they are still nothing
in themselves. By grace we are saved and by grace we
must live. Just as we came, saying, "Nothing in
my hand I bring," so we must live our Christian lives,
saying:

I'm only a sinner and nothing at all,
But Jesus Christ is my All in all.

The story of people who have been used greatly by
God is inevitably the story of those who learned one
way or another the lesson of humility. The average
Christian looks with awe upon the life of a man
like Moses, marveling at the way God was able to use
him. However, upon a close scrutiny of the story of
Moses, it can readily be seen that Moses' usefulness
resulted largely from his humility before God.

But Moses had to learn the lesson the hard way.
During the first forty years of his life in Egypt, Moses
was an important man. He wielded a great deal of
influence in the court. He was a man of worldly
prestige and power. In himself Moses was strong
enough to do a great deal for his brethren in captivity
and slavery. In those days, however, he was very
conscious of his own strength. He was aware of the
fact that he was a great man, and he knew that his
influence in the kingdom was far-reaching.

Realizing his own position of authority and
importance and seeing the apparent need of his
enslaved people, Moses decided to use his influence
to liberate them. This he proceeded to do. Just twice he
attempted to use his own power to relieve the strain

of bondage on the children of Israel, and almost immediately he was driven from Egypt to the land of Midian, where he dwelt in absolute ignominy for forty years. It was then that God spoke to him from the burning bush about the bondage of his people, and told him that he was to lead his people to freedom.

One can easily imagine what the response of the average modern pastor or evangelist would have been to such a commission: "Why, Lord, you've come to the right man this time. I've been waiting for this, and, Lord, I'm just the man you need to do the job. I have conducted scores of successful campaigns throughout Egypt and Midian. Thousands have made decisions as a result of my dynamic preaching. I play the trombone, sing solos, lead the singing, and play the sheep-bells. Just wait here, Lord, until I run home to my father-in-law's house and bring out some of my advertising material. We can take that down to Pharaoh, so he'll know I'm no ordinary person. We ought to send word on ahead for them to get the town band out and have the Lord Mayor give us his official welcome. Of course, Lord, we could hardly do anything unless that ungodly crowd of politicians down in Egypt gave us their official blessing..."

How different from this was Moses' response. In wide-eyed amazement he stood there, hardly believing his own ears, and simply said, "Who am I, that I should go?"

Yes, who was Moses? Moses was nobody that really counted in the world. Moses had no power of his own. He had no influence. His prestige was a thing of the past. There he was, out on the back side of the desert, a man who was nothing and knew it.

Then came God's answer—"Moses, it does not matter who you are. You go down into Egypt and tell the people who I am" (Exodus 3:12).

Oh, that God could find more people in this day and age humble enough when called to stand back in amazement and gasp, "Lord, who am I?" If only the religious leaders of today would come to the place spiritually where they would realize that in the work of God it does not matter who they are. What does matter is who God is. It is not a case of what any one person can do or has done. It is a case of what God can do and will do. Modern Christian workers sometimes send the fanfare of their own power ahead of them because they do not have the kind of faith it takes to depend completely upon the power of God. They would like to see the power of God demonstrated, but they are anxious for the world to know that *they* are the human instruments.

No one can possibly be the human leader of a revival without fulfilling this first condition, and no individual Christian can enjoy revival experience personally until he or she is humble before God.

"PRAY"

The second condition for revival is prayer, but we must conform to the divine order. Humility is first, prayer second. The second condition becomes effective only after the first is fulfilled. Prayer that does not stem from a life of humility before God is powerless and is little more than a waste of valuable time. It is only as Christians go down in humility before God that their prayers will rise and be effective.

Jesus gave an example of this in the story of the Pharisee and the publican. Both men prayed, but God answered only the prayer of the publican. In his own mind, the Pharisee prayed from an exalted position.

There he stood, in a public place where everybody could see him, and prayed, "God, I thank thee, that I am not as other men . . ." According to Jesus, God did not hear this prayer because the man lacked humility. The publican, on the other hand, standing afar off, apparently hoping that others would not see or hear him, cried out in deepest humbleness, "God be merciful to me a sinner." God answered this prayer because it stemmed from a heart of sincere humility (Luke 18:10-13).

Someone has proclaimed the truth that "prayer is the force that moves the hand that moves the world," and Tennyson adds, "More things are wrought by prayer than this world dreams of." However, the tragedy of most Christians' experience is that we forget that humility before God is the switch that turns on the power of prayer.

Sometimes as we read the stories of other days and the wonderful movement of the Spirit of God over large areas, the question arises, Why was there so much conviction of sin in those days and so little conviction of any kind today? The answer lies in the apparent deficiency in prayer power today. The history of revival proves that conviction comes as a result of the prayers of God's people. Where there is fervent prayer, there is deep conviction. Where there is no conviction, there is a lack of earnest prayer.

When Israel was to fight against Amalek, Joshua feared that his soldiers were not equal to the occasion. Amalek's armies were strong and his equipment was good. Humanly speaking, he should easily destroy the people of God. Joshua knew this and consulted Moses as to what he should do. Moses suggested a plan of operation and attack: "You take the army into battle against Amalek, and I will go with Aaron and

Hur up to the top of the mountain. There I will hold up the rod of the Lord while you fight the battle."

The rod of the Lord was indicative, of course, of Moses' contact with God, and as the story goes on this is what happened: as long as Moses maintained his contact with God, Joshua prevailed against Amalek; but when Moses grew weary toward the close of the day and let down the rod, losing his contact with God, Amalek prevailed against Joshua. Finally, with the assistance of Aaron and Hur, who supported the arms of Moses as he held the rod, Moses was able to renew and maintain his contact with God, and Joshua was victorious over Amalek (Exodus 17:8-13).

Joshua won the battle that day—not because he had a great army, or because he was a great military genius, or because he had better equipment than Amalek—but rather, because there were three men on the mountain-top of prayer who contacted God on his behalf.

It can happen in any church or in any service. If there are enough of God's people who have learned the secret of prevailing prayer and will covenant with one another and with God to uphold their minister in prayer as he proclaims the message, all the power of the world, the flesh, and the devil cannot hold back the blessing of God from that service.

There can never be a widespread revival until God's people have fulfilled the second condition. Humility before God must be coupled with fervent, gripping prayer if revival is to be realized in a church or in the life of an individual.

"SEEK"

Whenever the Lord was pleased with the conduct of the children of Israel, his pleasure was expressed by saying that his face was turned toward them. If the people were disobedient to the command of God, their disobedience caused him to turn his face away from them.

When Moses instructed Aaron how to bless the people, he told him to say, "The Lord make his face to shine upon thee," invoking the favor of God (Numbers 6:25). The Psalmist expressed the same idea when he said, "The eyes of the Lord are upon the righteous, and his ears are open unto their cry. The face of the Lord is against them that do evil" (34:15, 16). During a period of apostasy, when the people of Israel were very much in disgrace before God, Isaiah told them, "Your iniquities have separated between you and your God, and your sins have hid his face from you, that he will not hear" (Isaiah 59:2).

When God tells his people to seek his face, he is urging them to live in such a way that his face can be turned in their direction. Thus, they can enjoy the smile of the Lord because they are living in the center of his will. This is the third condition for revival. The Christian who is revived is the Christian who makes a habit of doing God's will.

The modern church says a great deal about following Jesus. We should certainly pattern our lives after that of our Lord. We should be like him in his kindness to others. We should be like him in his sympathy for others. We should try to the best of our ability to do as many good deeds as possible, and so on. But there is another aspect of the earthly life of the Lord in which it is absolutely necessary for every Christian to follow him; and while some follow him in one respect and others in another, the majority of Christians fail to follow him in this respect. While he was on this earth everything he did, every word he spoke, and every miracle or good deed that he performed was governed by one principle—"not my will, but thine." This was the guiding principle of his entire earthly life.

Perhaps the best example of this is found in his prayer in the Garden of Gethsemane. As he prayed he saw the "cup" before him and all that it involved—the sin of the world, the curse, hell, the cross, the shed blood, the grave, spiritual and physical death—and when he saw it all, the human part of him was repulsed by it. His human reaction was to turn away from the cross and the suffering that lay ahead and as he prayed, the humanity within him cried out to God, "If it be possible, let this cup pass from me." But even as he offered this prayer, the guiding principle of his life was brought into effect as he set his own will to one side and added, "Nevertheless, not as I will, but as thou wilt," and once more he subjected himself to the will of his Father (Matthew 26:39).

Christians who would follow the Lord Jesus Christ in any respect must follow him in this respect. We must lose sight of our own will and seek only to do the will of God. This is essential in the life of revived Christians, and the blessing of God can never rest upon the lives of those who have not fulfilled this third condition. As far as Christians are concerned, what they want to do does not count. What God wants them to do is important. What they wish to say means nothing. What God tells them to say is all that matters. Their ambitions, their aspirations, their desires, and their purposes in life must all take second place to the will of God. Their guiding principle must be that of their Lord—"Not my will, but thine be done."

Quite often people will tell Christian workers, "You are in the highest calling in the world. Why, to be a minister of the gospel, to be a missionary, to be in

full-time service for the Lord is the finest thing that
any man or woman could possibly do. There is no
greater calling than that of full-time service for God."

That is not true! The ministry is not the greatest
of Christian callings. The missionary is not necessarily
doing the most important work that can be done for
God. The young person who has gone into full-time
service may not be doing the most wonderful thing in
the world.

"But why?" you exclaim in amazement. "Everyone
has always agreed that there is no greater calling than
that of full-time Christian service. How can you say
it is not? Or if this is not the greatest of Christian
callings, what is?"

The most important thing that any child of God can
do is to live in the center of the will of God. That may
be behind the pulpit as a Christian minister. It could
be on the mission field as an evangelist or translator. It
might be in some form of full-time Christian service.
But it could also be behind the counter of a store as a
clerk. It could be on the seat of a tractor on a farm. It
could be in a home as a housewife, or in a school as a
teacher, or in a hospital as a nurse or a doctor, or in
a factory as a boilermaker, or on the roof of a house
as a carpenter. The essential thing is to make certain
that, whatever the work may be, it is the will of God
for the person concerned.

It is quite possible to be a minister and be out of
God's will. There have been missionaries who have
discovered that after all they were not in the will of
God. The full-time worker is in as much danger of
being out of the will of God as any layman.

To live according to the will of God is an essential
condition of revival. The revived Christian is one
who obeys God.

"TURN"

It is quite conceivable to think of people who have
fulfilled each of the first three conditions for revival,
but who are still lacking spiritual power because they
have never met the fourth condition. It might be
possible for Christians to be quite humble before the
Lord, to spend a great deal of time and energy in
prayer, and to read God's Word earnestly in an
endeavor to find God's purpose for life, and yet refuse
to turn from some form of sin, some habit, some
practice, some feeling, some weight that prevents
them from being completely revived Christians.

Some Christians are quite anxious to get right with
God, but never put forth any effort to get right
with people. They seem to think that it is possible to
have wrong relations with people and at the same
time have a right relation with God. They can bear a
grudge toward others as long as they have no grudge
against God. They can hate their fellows as long as
they love their God. They can live like sinners as long
as they think like saints. So they say!

God makes it clear that if revival is to be
experienced, there must be a turning from wickedness;
and if we are not willing to fulfill this final
condition for revival, we might just as well save the
energy and the time that it takes to meet the first
three. The Psalmist says, "If I regard iniquity in my
heart, the Lord will not hear me" (66:18). This means
that everything that is known to be wrong must go
if God is to send revival. The spirit of hatred must give
way to the spirit of love. The spirit of envy must
yield to the spirit of generosity. The spirit of competition
must step aside for the spirit of cooperation. The
spirit of jealousy must be replaced by the spirit of
fellowship. Open sins, secret sins, habits, and weights

must go if revival is to come.

These, then, are the conditions upon which God has promised to manifest his power and to hear the prayers of his people—humble, pray, seek, and turn. The four can be summed up in one simple sentence: "Get right with God." As far as eternal destiny is concerned, even the carnal Christian is right with God. But concerning fellowship and present living, he certainly is not. The Christian who is truly right with God is the Christian who is revived. The Christian who wants to be revived is the Christian who is willing to get right with God.

God has promised to do two things when the child of God meets these conditions. First, he will answer prayer—"I will hear from heaven." Second, he will manifest his power in the forgiveness of sin and the outpouring of his Spirit—"(I) will forgive their sin, and will heal their land." This, indeed, is revival.

Revival is not something for which we need to pray (though we should pray for sensitivity to sin, spiritual power and victory, etc.). Revival is something we can have, by obeying God. Revival is not something for which we must long and hope. Revival can be ours, now. In God's eyes, revival is not an unusual state for the children of God. Christians who are not revived are abnormal.

We may pray for revival in others and in our community and church. But as far as we personally are concerned, we simply fulfill the necessary conditions, get right with God, and so have revival in our own souls. Our prayer, then, should be, "Lord, as far as I know I am right with thee. Now begin to manifest thy power through me."

CHAPTER FOUR
WHAT REVIVAL DOES

Not all revivals are identical. Some things that occur in one do not occur in another. In fact, the characteristics of revivals are as varied as the revivals themselves. However, upon a study of the history of revival, it can be readily observed that there are a few fundamental characteristics common to most mass workings of the Spirit of God. If these things are not in evidence, there is probably no revival taking place.

UNITY OF BELIEVERS

One glaring proof that revival is still a great distance from most Christian communities is the very apparent lack of unity among believers. In revival, a given group of Christians is completely under the leadership of the Spirit of God. When such is the case, unity and fellowship among believers always results.

When Jesus came to earth he did two things. In the first place, he divided the world into two classes of people—those who believed in him and those who did not. In the second place, he united men and women from every walk of life, from every race, and from every heathen religion into one body of people of which he is the Head. "For he is our peace, who hath made both one, and hath broken down the middle wall of partition between us" (Ephesians 2:14).

People who would otherwise be separated from one another by barriers of all kinds are "made nigh" through the blood of Christ and are joined to one another and to their Lord in a bond of love. When Christians are right with God, as in a revival, the barriers that prevent them from having fellowship and cooperating with one another are broken down by the power of the indwelling Holy Spirit.

Barriers of Feeling. During a revival, barriers of feeling are broken down. Whereas there may be envy between Christians when there is no revival, when the Spirit of God has control envy is destroyed and communion takes its place. When there is no revival, there may be hatred among Christians; but when the Holy Spirit is in charge, love comes in and there is no room for hatred. Jealousy among God's people may be common when there is no revival, but under the dominating influence of the Spirit of God in days of revival jealousy has no part. One by one all the barriers of feeling that prevent us from working together and living together in peace are broken down as the Spirit takes control and regulates the activities of his people.

Barriers of Denomination. It has been the history of every revival that barriers of denomination are broken down as the Spirit of God gains complete dominion over his people. In many cases today Christians are more conscious of their affiliation with their church than they are of their association with their Lord. They may have a great deal to say about the cause of their own organization but very little to say about the cause of Christ. They are willing to back any effort that is put forth by their denomination, but they refuse to cooperate in any effort for God that may be put forth by some other denomination.

When there is no revival, many Christians are interested primarily in the progress of their own group; but in days of revival Christians are willing to let their own organization take second place to the cause of Christ, even if that cause is being advanced through the instrumentality of some other denomination. This has been true in the case of every revival. There is very little to be found in the story of revivals about any one denomination, but there is a great deal to be said about the movement of the Spirit of God in the living body of Christ which comprises all born-again people of all denominations.

There will be a day when denominations will be a thing of the past and the living church of Jesus Christ will stand as one united body of people linked together by a common bond of love for the Lord. Such a condition will be a reality in heaven, but it is also a reality upon earth whenever a group of Christian people is yielded fully to the leadership of the Holy Spirit. It has been the history of every revival that as Jesus Christ is exalted and the Holy Spirit assumes his rightful control of the Lord's people, the affiliations of this world become secondary. Christian people become conscious of the love that binds them together as one body in Christ.

This does not mean that denominations are not a necessity here on earth. They are absolutely essential to religious life and activity in this world. The variation of personality and character among Christian people demands a variety of outlets that will serve all types of people. That is why there are denominations. Without them the Christian church on earth could hardly function.

Barriers of Doctrine. Today there are multitudes of divisive doctrinal differences that prevent one Christian from working with another and thus destroy the unity of spirit and effort that there should be among Christians. When there is revival, these issues

are set to one side so that the cause of Christ
may go forward.

There are many things about which we disagree. The
differences of interpretation among Christians are
"legion." However, an investigation of the doctrines
upon which we differ will disclose the fact that in
nearly every case they involve issues that are
interesting and worthy of thought, but certainly not
of major importance.

It has been the history of the church during periods
of spiritual drought to allow secondary issues to
overshadow the essentials and become barriers to the
advance of the cause of Christ. In periods of revival the
emphasis is entirely different. As the church comes
under the dominating power of the Holy Spirit,
the barriers of doctrine that would otherwise separate
are broken down (or at least seen in true perspective)
and Christians unite behind the main cause.

Methods of church government, forms of baptism,
interpretations of prophecy, and other similar
doctrines would all serve as examples of those minor
issues that unrevived Christians allow to take a
major position in their thinking, a major portion of
their effort, and a major part of their time, and
thus result in a hindrance to the advance of the gospel.

Take the problem of Calvinism and Arminianism
as a case in point. For many years one branch of the
church has believed in the eternal security of the
believer, while another has maintained the belief that
it is possible for the Christian to fall from grace
and lose his salvation. Both groups quote Scriptures to
support their view. Both groups can mention the
names of many intelligent and well-educated
Christians who have embraced their particular
doctrinal position. Both groups can point out among

their leaders people of great spiritual stature who have accomplished much for God. When there is no revival, Christians who have lost their spiritual power bring up their side of the question and argue it belligerently as if it were of major importance, when in reality it may only be a sideline issue upon which greater minds than theirs have always disagreed.

As far as the believer is concerned, the essential issue is not one's relationship with God twenty-five years in the future, but, "Am I right with God now?" Many of us spend so much time and effort arguing about our future spiritual condition that we allow our present spiritual condition to suffer.

If we are certain of our contact with the Lord "moment by moment," we will not have to worry about our relationship to him in the future. The question of eternal security becomes nonessential as we face our immediate relationship with God. When there is no revival, this and other secondary issues are brought to the fore and succeed only in dividing the forces of Christianity and setting up barriers to the furthering of the Kingdom.

The cause of Christ can be summed up in one statement: to get the gospel to as many people as possible in the short time that remains. This is the first and most important task of the church. This is a truth to which any real Christian will assent. Most of the groups that differ on many of the unimportant doctrines agree on the one essential truth, "For God so loved the world, that he gave his only begotten Son, that whosoever believeth in him should not perish, but have everlasting life" (John 3:16). This is common ground for any born-again man or woman. To this the living body of Christ on earth assents. The person who does not believe this cannot be called a Christian.

Yes, this is the gospel to which every Christian must say "Amen." But the truth of the matter is that the lukewarm, unrevived, spiritually decadent members of the twentieth-century church seem to spend their time arguing and finding fault with one another over a lot of minor doctrines that do not amount to the proverbial "row of pins" or "hill of beans," while there are still thousands of unreached men and women who live in darkness because they have never heard that God loves them, that Jesus died for them, that there is One who can lift them out of their sin and misery and give them something for which to live and a future for which to hope.

Would to God that we would resolve to set aside our multitudinous divergencies of doctrinal interpretation and begin to unite our efforts and our prayers in a desperate drive to get the gospel to the whole world! It is time that some churches lost sight of their own petty little programs and caught a vision of the need of a sin-cursed world.

Is this organic church union? Most certainly it is not. It is the spirit of fellowship, cooperation, sympathy, and unity of a body of people who are driving toward a common goal in this life and who expect to live together in the life to come. Sadly, a fellowship of truly regenerate men and women in a united effort to proclaim the gospel that has made them one in Christ is a spiritual norm that has not often been attained.

When there is revival there is always unity. Where there is no unity there is still a crying need for revival.

PASSION FOR SOULS

In every revival Christian people have been driven

to activity by a burning passion for lost souls. That is one reason that so many sinners are born into the family of God during revival, even though the revival itself has to do with Christians. When Christian people are wholly yielded to God, the result inevitably seems to be that God gives them a passion to win lost men and women to Christ.

D. L. Moody attributed a great deal of his success as a soul-winner to the fact that God had given him a real love for people. He claimed that if he rebuked them he could not win them, if he criticized them he failed, if he condemned them they would not yield; but if he could convince them that D. L. Moody was sincerely interested in them—that he had a real love for them—half the battle was won. Thus Moody's untiring effort to win the lost stemmed from his great love for them. It was his love for souls that gave him his passion for souls.

It is so easy to do the Lord's work from a mere sense of responsibility. Many of us are driven to witness by a sense of obligation and nothing more, to win souls simply because we feel it is our duty as Christians to do so. How few are motivated by love for the lost. When mere obligation or sense of duty is the driving power behind Christian service, the results are always few; but when love becomes the propelling force, much fruit will be borne.

The daily prayer of every Christian should be, "O Lord, increase my love for lost souls." But love in itself is not sufficient. It is only as that love becomes a burden that activity will be the result.

There is one sense in which Christians should be the most carefree people in the world—our sins are forgiven and we are on our way to heaven; our future is secure. That is why Paul can urge Christians, as opposed to all other people, to "be careful [anxious] for nothing." But there is another very real sense in which Christians should be the most burdened people in the world, the most anxious people, weighted down with concern. We should be burdened about the lost condition of our friends. We should be loaded with care because of the peril in which the lost masses of the world lie.

How long has it been since you tossed through the hours of the night unable to sleep—not because of business problems, not because of domestic difficulties, not because of examinations that lie ahead, but because of a burden for some lost soul? Souls will not be won in any church unless its members have compassion for the lost. Souls will not be won by any individual Christian unless he shares God's love for people. The unsaved will be reached for Christ in any community only in proportion to the concern that the Christians of that community have for the lost.

In our daily prayer we should go one step further and ask the Lord to take the love and the burden and ignite them into a passion within our hearts that will drive us out into the field of active service. In revival there is always a passion for the lost. In the hearts of revived Christians, there will be a compulsion to reach lost souls.

Nothing will give the personal worker or the Sunday school teacher or the preacher a greater concern for the lost than a realization of the issues at stake, issues set forth clearly and unmistakably in the book of Deuteronomy: "I call heaven and earth to record this day against you, that I have set before you life and death, blessing and cursing: therefore choose life, that both thou and thy seed may live" (30:19).

This was the final warning of Moses to the people during the last year of his life. It is followed by a long song that would always remind the Israelites of God's grace in their history and the importance of listening to and obeying his law. The whole import of the warning is that their relationship to God was a matter of life and death.

These are the eternal issues that are at stake every time the message of the gospel is proclaimed to an individual or a group. If we were simply trying to persuade people to assent to a different set of beliefs, there would be no need for passion. If we were presenting nothing more than a new philosophy of life in a world where there are already thousands of others, we would not need to be insistent. But when we realize that every time we open our mouths to witness for Christ, we are giving the person before us a choice between blessing and cursing, between life and death, between heaven and hell, how can we help but be urgent in our appeal?

When there is a revival, Christian people who are brought under the dominating influence of the Holy Spirit will have a passion for souls.

EFFECTIVE TESTIMONY

Quite often when there is no revival a great many words bring very few results. Much preaching bears little fruit. Testimony is ineffective. When there is revival, testimony takes on an effectiveness that it has never had before. As the lives of Christians yield to the power of the Holy Spirit, the testimony of their lips becomes secondary as the testimony of their lives gains new power. When there is revival in the hearts of Christians, few words often bring many results and little preaching bears much fruit.

As we shall observe in another chapter, Charles G. Finney, the American revivalist who was perhaps the foremost leader of a series of revivals dating from about 1821 through 1868, connects his "baptism of the Holy Ghost" directly with his conversion. The interesting outcome of his experience, and of the beginnings of the revival movement, was the immediate effectiveness of his life and testimony. In his autobiography he tells about his contacts within a day or two of his conversion and baptism: "I spoke with many persons that day and I believe the Spirit of God made lasting impressions upon every one of them. I cannot remember one whom I spoke with, who was not soon after converted."[1]

In every revival history there are many similar stories of effective testimony. As Christians are revived self is forgotten, Christ is lifted up, and the exaltation of the Lord in the lives of his people gives their testimony a power that cannot be duplicated without revival.

The eleventh chapter of John's Gospel tells how Jesus raised Lazarus from the dead. The news spread quickly and reached the ears of the chief priests and the Pharisees. Fearing the growing popularity of Jesus as a result of his most recent and greatest miracle, they made plans to put him to death.

Six days before the Passover, when the plot for the abduction and crucifixion of Jesus was apparently almost complete, the chief priests received word of a new menace to their power.

Jesus had returned to the home of Mary, Martha, and Lazarus, and as usual a great crowd of the common

1. Finney, Charles G., *Memoirs of Charles G. Finney* (New York: Fleming H. Revell Company, 1876), p. 26.

people had made their way to the place, not only to see Jesus but also to see Lazarus whom he had raised from the dead. The new problem was that many of the people who went up to Bethany no sooner saw Lazarus, and realized what the Lord had done for him, than they went away believing on Jesus.

When the conspirators heard this, they immediately began to plot the death of Lazarus also, for they realized that whether they succeeded in putting Jesus to death or not, as long as Lazarus was alive he would be a living testimony of Jesus' power. The Lord had wrought such a miracle in the experience of Lazarus that as long as he lived, he would lead all who saw him to believe in Jesus—and if the testimony of Jesus was to be silenced, the life of Lazarus would have to be taken.

"Much people of the Jews therefore knew that he was there: and they came not for Jesus' sake only, but that they might see Lazarus also, whom he had raised from the dead. But the chief priests consulted that they might put Lazarus also to death; because that by reason of him many of the Jews went away, and believed on Jesus" (John 12:9-11).

What a glorious thing it would be if every Christian could be a modern Lazarus! The Lord gave Lazarus new physical life. How much more he has done for thousands since that time! To every Christian Jesus has imparted eternal life—divine life. How much greater a testimony to the power of God should the modern Christian be even than the resurrected Lazarus!

When we are right with God—truly revived—saved and victorious—we can expect God to demonstrate his power through our lives in such a way that people, after looking at us, will go away believing on Jesus.

This is effective testimony. This is characteristic of the revived Christian. When there is revival, testimony that has never borne fruit will become effective. When testimony is powerless, there is no revival.

INFLUX OF THE UNSAVED

The church may not necessarily produce a better program, greater singer, more eloquent speaker, or more gifted musician than the world already has, nor is it the responsibility of the church to do so. But the church can present to the world a Savior. This is its task, and this is the only field in which the world cannot compete—and this is the only way that the church can ever hope to attract unchurched people. Although the program may not attract them, the Lord Jesus Christ will. The music may have no power to draw them, but the Savior will. Many non-Christians are not impressed by an eloquent speaker, but if they see an exalted Christ, they will know they need him.

That is why the history of every revival tells the story of a great influx of the unconverted. When there is a revival, church programs and personnel are eclipsed as Jesus is lifted up. The world is hungry for him and if they are going to flock to anything religious, it will be to hear an honest, exciting, and realistic presentation of the claims of Jesus Christ.

How the church can thank God for everyone who is proclaiming the gospel! How fortunate the Christians of this era are that so many have given their musical and artistic and technical talent to the Lord! What a privilege it is for an evangelist to go into a campaign that has been well organized and highly advertised!

But oh, how every Christian worker needs to pray for the grace through it all to exalt the Lord Jesus Christ. It is only then that the unsaved will be attracted.

When there is revival, the unconverted flock to hear the Word of God. If this isn't happening, there is probably no revival happening either.

EFFICIENT LIVING

The reason for the interest of the unsaved during a revival (this is closely aligned with the effective testimony of Christians affected by revival) is that for the first time in many cases the people of the world see Christians who are living efficiently for Christ.

Efficiency is the keynote of this age. Men and women in every profession and trade are striving toward perfection as perhaps never before.

That is why there is so much specialization. Very few people attempt to master an entire field. Most doctors study the human body in a general sort of way, but do not feel properly equipped to cope with the competition in the practical field until they have segregated some small part of the subject and "specialized" in it. Modern engineers are never merely engineers. Rather they are known as a mechanical, electrical, aeronautical, or some other specific type of engineer. Even a person in a trade specializes. One person does not tailor an entire suit, build a complete car, or manufacture a whole piece of furniture. It takes a host of workers, each doing a minute part of the work on an assembly line, to produce the finished article.

Such a system tends to develop a group of workers who, although their field is extremely limited, do a very efficient piece of work. The person who is unable to maintain a high level of performance finds it difficult to keep his job.

As we see this surge of unregenerate people toward efficiency, the question that should force itself upon our minds is this: "Am I striving as strenuously toward perfection in my service for the Lord Jesus Christ as the people of the world are in their service to Satan? Am I living as efficiently for God as unsaved people are for themselves?"

The only answer that can be given to such questions in most cases is "No!" A casual glance at the condition of the Christian church reveals at once why this is so.

In the early days of church history, there was only a small group of Christian people. The "believers" in the days recorded by Luke in the book of Acts could be numbered without difficulty—a few thousand at the most. But despite the weakness of their numbers, Christians were referred to as "these that have turned the world upside down" (17:6).

Today church statistics go into the millions. Yet with all our numerical force we are not making one-tenth the impact on this age as a few thousand did in the early years of church history.

The comparison forces today's Christians in most cases to admit failure. If we were efficient, the world would feel the impact. But the truth is that we are noticed little more than a pinprick on the hide of an elephant, or a .22 caliber bullet in the forehead of a buffalo.

The church is not effective because too many of her professed members are playing with Christianity instead of living it. Many a Christian's faith is more of a game than a warfare. Love for the Lord is frigid and lifeless rather than passionate and vital. We toy with the ethics of the Man of Galilee without taking up the cross of the God of Calvary.

We play while the world does business. We mark
time and the world marches forward. We are content
to stagnate and see the world flow over and beyond us.
We are satisfied that we have reached our limit,
but the world sees no limit. We are inefficient in a
world which is ever straining toward greater efficiency.
We possess a prize which the wealth of the world
cannot buy, but we are playing with it.

See how we play!

The average Christian goes through life dividing it
into two parts. On one side of life is written the
heading "secular" and under it there are a great many
things—business, social life, recreation, friendships,
education, family, home, etc. On the other side of
life is written the word "sacred," and under that
heading he lists church, Sunday school, choir, family
altar, etc.

Suppose that a Christian falls deeply in love with a
girl. Immediately he finds himself completely
engrossed with her. He thinks of her day and night.
He becomes fanatically interested in every detail
of her life. He has an unquenchable thirst to know
everything about her. He wants her to share even the
most precious and closely guarded secrets of her
heart, and he is slighted if she refuses.

All of this, although a new experience to the young
man, is not an unusual thing. Those who have loved
deeply and devotedly have enjoyed the same
experience, for love always demands the whole being
and a share in every interest of the beloved's life.
Love is extremely possessive.

But this is an attribute of mere human love. Now,
consider the love of God. Surely it surpasses in every
way the love of any man for a woman. The Bible
proclaims the fact that his love is greater than the love

of a father who pities his children and deeper than
the love of a mother who nurses her child.

If human love demands all, surely divine love must
have all as well (though unselfishly). If finite love
concerns itself over details, infinite love must be
infinitely concerned about the most minute details of
our lives. If the Christian is interested in every
part of his beloved's life, how much more must God be
interested in every phase of the Christian's life.

If this be so, there can be no such thing as a secular
side of life for the Christian. For the child of God,
all of life must be sacred, sacred because God's love
takes an interest in it.

Until we can write the one word *sacred* in bold
letters over every phase of life, every business
transaction, every friendship, every social engagement,
every enterprise, every recreation, we must admit
that we are still playing with Christianity. It has never
become vital. It has never shattered the veneer of
our profession and made us the possessors of a faith for
which we would die.

See again how we play!

It is a paradox to say so, but there is probably more
truthful lying done in the hymn-singing on Sunday
morning in church than anywhere else. Many
Christians are truthful because they sing sincerely,
but they lie because they do not fulfill their vows. We
sing the old hymns of the church, and as we sing we
wish with all our hearts that we could rise to the
heights of devotion, loyalty, and service about which
we are singing; but as we go out of the church to live
in the world, our actions often turn our words
into lies.

With all the sincerity we can muster we will sing
the old hymn

Oh, for a thousand tongues
To sing my great Redeemer's praise!

And when we sing, a cry seems to go up from the
depths of our souls to God that we might have the
"thousand tongues" to tell the world about the One

Who breaks the power of cancelled sin,
And sets the pris'ner free.

But when Monday morning comes we are hesitant
to use one tongue to tell fellow-workers about the
Lord, let alone use a thousand if we had them.
  We sing the great hymn of consecration:

When I survey the wondrous Cross
On which the Prince of Glory died,
My richest gain I count but loss,
And pour contempt on all my pride.

But when Missionary Sunday gives us an
opportunity to prove our consecration, we are usually
unwilling to give God one-tenth of our "richest
gain," let alone turn over to him everything that
belongs to him.
  Or perhaps we declare our loyalty to Jesus Christ in
the words of the old hymn of the cross:

Must Jesus bear the Cross alone,
And all the world go free?
No, there's a cross for ev'ry one,
And there's a cross for me.

The consecrated cross I'll bear,
'Til death shall set me free;

And then go home my crown to wear,
For there's a crown for me.

Thank God—for faithful servants of the Lord, there
is a crown at the end of the road. But so often we
take up the cross as we sing the hymn only to leave it
on the church steps as we go out. We are willing to
carry the cross into the Sunday school class, but are
ashamed to bear it in the public school or university.
We glory in the cross as we stand in the choir loft and
sing the anthem, but we are ashamed to uphold the
cross in the business office. We bear the cross on
Sunday, but Monday through Saturday the cross is
foreign to us.

There are so many Christians today who seem to
have forgotten the conditions of discipleship. What did
Jesus ask of the men whom he called to follow
him? Is this the story as it is found in the Bible?

Jesus was walking along by the Sea of Galilee one
day, and there by the shore he found some fishermen
mending their nets. He stopped to talk to them.

"In just a little while I am going to ride through
Jerusalem, and I would like some of you to come
with me.

"About a mile from here I have a bandwagon all
ready to go. It's decorated with flags and banners, and
I have hired six white chargers to pull it. Will you
come with me?"

The men began to look interested as this strange
Man continued.

"The band is ready to play. At the blast of the bugle
and the beat of the drum we will be off, through
the streets of Jerusalem. Will you come?"

Their eyes began to sparkle; they let the nets slip

slowly from their fingers as they edged forward
to hear him, but no one spoke.

"And as we ride through the main street of the city,
every knee will bow before us. The people will
applaud and cheer. We will be exalted to the very
heavens among them. No honor will be too great, no
service too difficult. On and on we will be carried on
the crest of the wave of public favor, and the end
will not be reached until we have established a
kingdom that will be greater and more glorious than
Solomon's.

"I will be the King and you, you humble fishermen,
will be my ministers of state. Now, answer me! Are
you ready to mount the bandwagon with me and
ride through Jerusalem?"

Is this the record as it appears in the New
Testament? No, it is far from the truth. Of course,
the conversation is not given in detail, but if all the
information in the Gospels were to be compiled the
story would read something like this:

Jesus did walk along the Sea of Galilee one day, and
there, coming upon some fishermen mending their
nets, he paused to talk to them. The nets slipped
quickly from their hands as he began to speak.

"In a very short time I am going to enter Jerusalem
and ride through the streets. I would like you to
come with me."

There was a restlessness among the men. Their
interest was aroused and they moved forward to listen.

"I do not have a bandwagon. There will be no flags,
no banners, no white chargers. A poor farmer has
offered me the use of his unbroken colt, and I will ride
it into the city. I do not want to go alone; I want

some of you, or all of you, to follow me. Will you come?"

There was a shuffle as a great giant of a man rose and began to clamber over the side of the boat, eager to follow the Lord. But Jesus held up his hand and stopped him, and then continued, "Before you come with me, I want you to consider the cost. Do not be like the man who began to build his house but lacked the bricks to finish it. Make sure you have enough bricks of character and backbone to complete the task. Or be not as the one I saw by the wayside who turned from his plow at the stroke of the dinner hour while yet his furrow was but half plowed. Do not follow me unless you are ready to plow through to the end of the row."

But somehow these men did not seem to hear his words. Their eyes were fixed on his face. There was something there that seemed to draw them—a depth in those eyes that captivated their very souls and made them feel that they could easily die for this Man. Their nets and their needles were forgotten. Eagerly they leaned forward, gripping the gunwale of the boat. Their eyes glistened with anticipation as they waited for a second invitation to follow him. But it did not come. Instead he only warned them further.

"There will be no positions of state for you. No one will applaud you. The world will not honor you nor sing your praises. They will find fault with you and ridicule you. They will make it difficult for you, put obstacles in your way, call you fools; and when I leave they will persecute you, and if the opportunity arises they will kill you."

There was a pause. The men looked at one another and then turned back to look again at that face and at those eyes, so deep and sorrowful, and yet so impelling. And they waited breathlessly for the invitation—to die for him if need be.

"If any man will come after me, let him deny himself, and take up his cross, and follow me" (Matthew 16:24).

And those words ring down through the centuries. The invitation is still open, and it is still the same. He who would become a disciple must fulfill the conditions. Christianity is not a bandwagon but a cross!

Christians who have never suffered for their Lord, those who have never been ridiculed for their faith, those who have never felt the lash of the world's hatred nor the sting of its contempt have never really bent under the burden of the cross—and must admit that they have been playing with Christianity. They have never come out boldly and taken a firm stand for the Lord Jesus Christ.

Is it not time for us to stop playing and begin living? Is there not a need to go beyond superficiality and nominalism and grapple with reality? Should we not drop our toys by the wayside and take up our cross? Can we be content with our imperfections when by the power of God we could be mature and strong?

The world is efficient for itself. God help the church to be efficient for him! Revival produces effective Christians, Christians who startle the world— sometimes even toward Christ.

REALITY

When there is no revival, Christians have a tendency to put up a sort of spiritual camouflage and as a result lack the one characteristic of faith and life that can convince the most stubborn unbeliever—reality.

Christian Experience. Sadly, many professing Christian people have never had any real experience with the Lord Jesus Christ. Too many have aligned themselves with the church for what they think they may get out of it. Such membership is quite popular in many areas of our country, a status or prestige symbol. Often this enables social contacts that would be impossible otherwise. In many cases it is looked upon as good for business to have a church connection. Or sometimes it is simply a national or family tradition that has filled the church roll.

Such people have no real interest in the things of God. There is little concern for their own spiritual welfare and, of course, not much for the souls of others. They lack that inner driving force that comes only as a result of a real experience of salvation. As long as it is popular, beneficial, and does not cost them anything by way of sacrifice, they will remain; but when the going gets hard, when the testing comes, when sacrifice is necessary, they are the first to withdraw.

It would be a blessing to the church and a favor to the people themselves if the membership could be purged of them. A policy of "prove your faith or put in your resignation" would do a great deal to bring revival to the modern church.

But where does it start? How can the members who really mean business be separated from those who have never had a real experience?

Of course no rigid line can be drawn. Only God himself could draw an accurate line between the real and the unreal. However, in some cases it is obvious that even a Sunday school scholar could do it. First, cross off everybody who only puts in an appearance on Easter Sunday or Christmas. There is little doubt that those who are not interested enough to attend the house of God except on special occasions have never had any real experience of salvation.

Cross off all the choir members, board members, Sunday school teachers, youth workers, deacons, elders, and stewards that *never* attend the prayer meeting. These people would appear to be lacking in any real spiritual interest. Most Christians miss some of the prayer meetings, but no one who misses all of them should claim to be much of a Christian and certainly is of little value to the church. (Obviously there are valid exceptions, such as the elderly with severe physical limitations, etc.)

I realize that I have written these lines leaving the impression that it is somebody's duty to go about the church acting as if they were God—making arbitrary judgments about fellow Christians. We have too many of these self-appointed judges in our churches already, and in a later chapter I have talked in more detail about the danger of crossing other people off.

However, what we are discussing here is a very biblical concept. Purging of the church roll should not be objective in most cases but rather subjective. There may be times when church discipline will have to be exercised by the spiritual leaders of our group, but they will be few and far between—the exception, not the rule.

The Apostle Paul teaches that we should have the courage to judge ourselves: "Let a man examine himself . . . for if we would judge ourselves, we should not be judged" (1 Corinthians 11:28, 31). This has nothing to do with our salvation, but it is very much to the point here because it is a self-examination to see if we are prepared for the fellowship of the Lord's

Table. A similar examination should be made in connection with our right to call ourselves church members or church officeholders.

We could also mention 2 Corinthians 13:5— "Examine yourselves, whether ye be in the faith."

It is not enough to be affiliated in a technical way with some church. It is essential to have had a real personal experience with the Son of God. It would deplete the ranks of the church sorely to adopt the policy just outlined, but oh, how much stronger would the remnant be, and how much greater impact could it make on the world!

Christian Living. After each child of God has been able to answer satisfactorily the question, "Have I had a real Christian experience?" the next burning question should be, "Am I demonstrating the reality of my experience in my Christian living?"

Perhaps the most widely used excuse of the unsaved person is, "He's a fine preacher, but he does not practice what he preaches—a good deacon, but I wouldn't want to do business with him—a diligent worker in the women's missionary society, but I live next door to her, and I'm not interested in her brand of Christianity—a faithful alto in the choir, but anything but a real Christian in her home life, claiming to have had a real experience with God, but living the life of a hypocrite."

True, this is no excuse for sinners—they will still have to answer for themselves before God—but what a sad indictment upon the church that so many of us leave room for such criticism from the world. What an impact could be made upon the unsaved if only everyone who claims a real Christian experience would back it up by the testimony of a truly Christian life!

It is one thing to have the light of the gospel within; it is another thing to "let your light so shine before men, that they may see your good works, and glorify your Father which is in heaven" (Matthew 5:16). That is why Jesus urged his disciples not to hide their light under a bushel. The Apostle Paul saw the same need in the church at Ephesus when he wrote, "For ye were sometimes darkness, but now are ye light in the Lord: walk as children of light" (Ephesians 5:8).

It is one thing to have access to the power of God; it is quite another to demonstrate that power to the world by the testimony of a life that is consistently Christian. As long as the engine is standing in the railway station, the engineer may talk endlessly about its ability to pull the long line of cars down the track at tremendous speed; but no one is convinced of the truth of his statements until he climbs into the cab and pulls the throttle that hitches the power to the wheels—and the train begins to move. The trouble with most Christians is that they have never hitched the power of God to the wheels of their everyday lives.

The world can only see the light that shines, the power that acts, and the faith that works. That was the crying need of the church of James' day, when the Spirit of God inspired him to declare, "Faith, if it hath not works, is dead" (James 2:17).

Christian Service. Finally, if Christians are to have the kind of testimony that they should have in the world, there must not only be reality in Christian experience and in Christian living, but there must also be reality in Christian service.

Many Sunday school teachers must confess a sad lack of reality in their teaching. They stay out late on Saturday night and then tumble into bed without any preparation for the lesson. Still weary, they rise in the morning with just enough time for a hasty cup of coffee and slice of toast and hurry out of the house with their quarterlies under their arms, intending to read as much as possible during the twenty minute ride that takes them to the church and to their classes.

As they sit through the opening exercises, they hope the singing will run long and thus cut the teaching period short. As the roll is taken after the class has assembled, Johnny's measles and Mary's mumps are discussed at length, further infringing on the lesson period. As a last resort a prayer session is held and as many as possible are urged to pray, again robbing precious moments from the instruction, and finally the lessons start. But because there has been no preparation, the teachers begin with the list of questions to be found at the end of every lesson and manage to drag them out until they're saved by the bell. Thus the hungry hearts of boys and girls go home with no more spiritual food to carry them through the coming week than they had before they came to Sunday school. Is it any wonder, then, that seven out of eight people stop Sunday school attendance before they reach fifteen years of age?

Many choir members exhibit the same lack of seriousness in their singing. Quite often it is merely love for music rather than love for God that is the motivating force. In many cases it is the position before the congregation, nourishing the fleshly desire to be seen and appreciated, that keeps them in the choir rather than their desire to get the message of the gospel across to the hungry hearts of men and women in the pews.

Only eternity will ever be able to tell the story of the multitudes that have been drawn to the Savior through voices of people who meant business for God as they sang—people who were genuine in their Christian service.

The same could be said about the elder, the deacon, the board member, the organist, the usher, and the custodian. What a need there is for children of God to demonstrate the reality of our experience and the reality of our lives by the reality of our Christian service!

Jeremiah saw the need in his day and cried out his protest; Jesus was aware of the same deficiency and condemned it in the Pharisees and Sadducees; the Apostle Paul was aware of it. Each in turn exposed it, but as one looks back along the corridors of time, it seems that there has never been such an alarming dearth of reality as there is today.

Would to God that each of us would search our own hearts, making certain that we have had a real experience with God, that our experience is being demonstrated every day to the world by obedient Christian lives, and that our service to God rings clear with a note of genuineness and power that is unmistakable.

This then is revival. These are some of the results that should be expected. Without them the church tends to be "blind, halt, withered, and quite impotent" in its attempts to reach the world. The waters are troubled as they were at Bethesda, but the church is helpless to get into the pool. It will take the Holy Spirit to overflow the water on the church. This will be revival!

PART TWO

The Challenge of the Church: Gifts of the Spirit

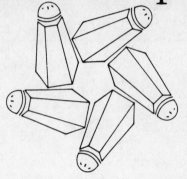

CHAPTER FIVE
GIFTS OF THE SPIRIT— USED OR ABUSED?

The church of Jesus Christ is not only made up of individuals who have had personal encounters with Christ. The church is a *community* of God's people, called to an eternity of worship and service.

The Greek word translated "church" in the New Testament is *ekklesia* (literally, an assembly of citizens called out). The Old Testament (and thus Hebrew) equivalent is *qahal*, used to refer to the people of Israel when assembled for religious purposes. (Theologically, however, there was no "church" until the Day of Pentecost when the Holy Spirit incorporated the New Testament people of God into one body.)

To be a member of the one true church of God is to be a member of a divine community. This is seen throughout the New Testament (Matthew 18:17; Ephesians 5:27; 1 Timothy 3:15; etc.).

No denomination or single group of worshipers is synonymous with *the* church. As John D. Jess has written:

The Body of Christ is more than a group of likeminded people, electing officers, calling a minister, and filing for tax-exempt status. Some such institutions are little more than social clubs, recreational centers, or local societies. Membership costs nothing in the way of personal piety. They are only convenient places to hold bingo parties and throw social wingdings.

The true *Church is a universal body of believers who have received Jesus Christ into their hearts and lives and who recognize Him as their Head, their sole Authority and their living Lord.*

. . . The true Church, you see, is a fellowship *composed of born-again believers in Jesus Christ. It may be preferable, but it is not essential that they be organized and incorporated, for the Church is not a building, it is not a membership, it is not a form of worship, it is not a denomination. The Church consists of believers, or Christ-accepters, or Christians (Christ's ones). . . .*

The true *Church is composed of people of all nationalities. The color of one's skin, his ethnic origin, his geographical location, or his religious background has nothing to do with his membership in this worldwide brotherhood.*

When the Spirit of God is allowed to function within the hearts and lives of believers within the true Church, there is evidenced a warmth of fellowship and love unequalled in any other facet of society. [1]

This is not to say that there should be no church in the popular sense of the word. There is strong scriptural support for an assembly of believers which is organized and meets in a specific geographical location at definite times on special days. The gifts of the Spirit would have little value if fellow Christians did not meet consistently with one another so their various gifts could in fact operate in edifying one another. The gifts do not work in a vacuum, nor in an invisible assembly. Much of the New Testament was written initially to assemblies of Christians, called

1. John D. Jess, *Let's Talk about the Church* (booklet) (Wheaton, Ill.: Chapel of the Air).

churches, which met in very definite geographical locations.

The Holy Spirit indwells his church (John 14:16,17), performing spiritual ministries essential for the health and strength of the people of God. He teaches us (John 16:13-15), gives us spiritual power (Acts 2), develops godliness in us (Galatians 5:22, 23), prays on our behalf (Romans 8:26).

In addition, the Spirit of God equips us to serve Christ. God never commands us to do anything without providing us the wisdom, ability, and power needed to perform that task. Does God want you to witness to a disinterested or even hostile relative? He will also give you the necessary boldness and wisdom. Is the Lord asking you to have a ministry of one kind or another in the inner city? Ask him for the courage you lack; he will supply it generously. Has God made it plain that you should help with your church's visitation program? He can bring you the self-control and discipline without which you just "don't have the time" to get involved.

One way the Spirit equips us is by giving each one of us (not only the clergy, not only the super-talented, not only the long-time Christians—see 1 Peter 4:10, 11) special abilities, spiritual gifts to use in serving him. We don't all have the same gifts, but none of us is left out. The main passages telling us about this are Romans 12:3-8, 1 Corinthians 12—14, and Ephesians 4:11, 12.

An understanding of the Holy Spirit and the ways he works in and among us is absolutely essential for efficient Christian living. Without the Holy Spirit there can be no revival, no spiritual victory, no continuing growth in us.

Unfortunately, at this point we lose each other in a

semantic jungle. Though we don't usually admit it, we are often talking about the same thing. Some prefer to speak about "the baptism of the Spirit" or of the Holy Ghost; others refer to "the Spirit-filled life" or "the victorious Christian life." In Holiness groups, words like "sanctification" and "perfection" are popular. Others insist on expressions such as "Christian growth" or "maturity." Obviously, we should not and cannot say one phrase is best and others should be discarded. Different terminology merely reflects a slightly different slant or perspective. If we're going to be honest about it, we have to admit that all these expressions mean basically the same thing, and so all are acceptable.

Although there may be nuances of meaning in these expressions, we all agree that all Christians become the dwelling place of the Holy Spirit at the time of their conversion or new birth. The Bible is quite clear about this: "Now if any man have not the Spirit of Christ, he is none of his. . . . But if the Spirit of him that raised up Jesus from the dead dwell in you . . ." (Romans 8:9-11). Indeed, it would be difficult to make much sense out of the eighth chapter of Romans without accepting the fact that believers are indwelled by the Holy Spirit. People who have been saved never need to ask the Holy Spirit to come into their lives. He is already there.

Differences between Christians usually arise in connection with our relationship to the Holy Ghost *after* he came into our lives when we accepted Christ as our Savior. The Bible does command us to "be filled with the Spirit." In our word-pictures of a "filling," we generally think of something on the outside being poured into a container until it is full. But the Holy Spirit is not outside the believer,

waiting to be poured in. He is inside, waiting for us to
invite him to flow through every area of our lives and
fill us—much as a gas in the physical world might be
released from inside a building and expand until
it fills the entire building.

I prefer to use the word "control"—"be controlled
by the Spirit." As we yield ourselves more and
more to him, he exercises greater control of us,
increasing godliness in us.

Most Christians would not object to these basic
facts about our relationship to the Holy Spirit. Yet we
quarrel over the vocabulary we use to describe our
experience, and even become more dogmatic and
vocal when we start discussing the results of this
experience. If we are submitting to the Spirit, should
there be some dramatic evidence in the form of a
miraculous spiritual gift? More specifically, will
contact with the Spirit always bring at least one
experience of speaking in tongues?

Let me say right here that I am not claiming that
tongues is the most important gift, or the least
important, or that speaking in tongues is the central
issue. I realize that because I am devoting quite
a few pages to the gift of tongues, I may be accused by
some of blowing this particular subject out of
proportion. I don't think I am.

The reason I am somewhat dwelling on tongues is
simply because I feel this particular topic is in several
ways a typical issue, and that our attitudes toward
it will match our attitudes toward other issues having
to do with the gifts of the Spirit.

At one time the gift of tongues was discussed only
among our Pentecostal Christian brethren. These
brothers and sisters often referred to the "baptism of
the Holy Ghost" as something that takes place

subsequent to salvation, a "second blessing." (Many Pentecostals still believe that speaking in tongues is the one necessary evidence that this experience has really taken place. If you have received the baptism, you have spoken in tongues. If you have never spoken in tongues, there is no proof that you have received the baptism. At some public meetings and most "after meetings," many Pentecostal churches today encourage speaking in tongues and create an atmosphere in which it would seem the natural and expected thing for possessors of this gift to do.)

This seemed to make dialogue between Pentecostals and non-Pentecostals quite clear. Everybody knew the ground rules, and it was simply a case of supporting one view or the other with a sound exegesis of Scripture. (Somehow both groups seemed to have solid scriptural backing for their interpretations!) In the following chapters, in which I have dealt with every passage in the Bible that refers to speaking in tongues, I have tried to give a sound exposition of the verses involved and have addressed myself to these essential questions: Is tongues the only necessary evidence of the "baptism" or "filling" of the Holy Spirit; and, how should the gift of tongues be used in a public service? I am aware of the fact that Pentecostals distinguish tongues as an evidence from tongues as a gift. However, I do not think this alters the argument seriously.

When Pentecostals and charismatics talk about the "baptism of the Holy Ghost," they are describing what most other Christians would call the "filling of the Spirit"—i.e., any crisis experience subsequent to salvation that began a Christian life recognizing and yielding to the power of the Holy Spirit.

In my opinion, the word "baptism" in the Scriptures

does not refer to a "second work of grace." Of course, most often the word is connected with the ordinance of water baptism. However, John the Baptist did prophesy that Jesus would "baptize you with the Holy Ghost, and with fire" (Matthew 3:11). Whatever else this involves in the Gospel accounts, two of them (Matthew and Luke) seem to me to indicate that the baptism of the Spirit includes separating the wheat from the chaff, consummating in final judgment. Many charismatics agree that the gathering of the wheat pictures salvation, whereas the "second blessing" involves people who have already been saved. All of the other Gospel writers quote John's prophecy in more or less the same words (Mark 1:8; Luke 3:16, 17; John 1:33).

This prophecy, referred to several times in the book of Acts (2:1-11; 10:44-48; 19:1-6), is interpreted in at least two ways. Traditionally, commentators have assumed that each of these Acts incidents involved the first advent of the Holy Spirit on the early Christians and that what took place—as on the Day of Pentecost—"baptized" these people into the body of Christ, the church. (This is what the baptism of John did not do, and it is John's baptism to which this new baptism was always compared. John's was a baptism for repentance, and he was doing it even before Christ appeared on the scene.)

The Apostle Paul seems to define the baptism of the Holy Ghost in this way—"For by one Spirit are we all baptized into one body" (1 Corinthians 12:13). Although this is one of the chapters where he deals with the dramatic gifts of the Spirit and tongues in particular, by no sound exposition could this verse be made to apply to anything but the initial experience of salvation when we become a part of the body of

Christ. His use of the word "baptism" in Galatians 3:27 and Romans 6:3 would lead to the same conclusion.

An alternative interpretation of John's prophecy would be that the baptism of the Holy Ghost is an experience that may take place after salvation. This seems to be supported by the examples in Acts where the people involved were already believers, but were ignorant of the teaching about the Holy Spirit. When they learned about the Spirit, they had a "second work of grace" or a "second blessing" as they were baptized by the Holy Ghost. Personally, I feel that these people were being added by "the baptism of the Holy Ghost" to the body of Christ at this time.

I think it is somewhat confusing to make "the baptism of the Spirit" synonymous with "the filling of the Spirit," or any phrase that describes a second work of grace type of experience. I do not feel that biblically these two are the same at all.

I do not always agree with the interpretations and outlines of the Scofield Bible, but I think its exegesis of the passages on the baptism of the Holy Spirit are true to the intent of the Scriptures:

Every believer is born of the Spirit (John 3:3-6; I John 5:1); indwelt by the Spirit, whose presence makes the believer's body a temple (I Corinthians 12:12-13; I John 2:20, 27), thus sealing him for God (Eph. 1:13; 4:30). [2]

In the Scofield Bible, the four Gospel records of the prophecy of John the Baptist refer us to the note on Acts 2:4. In other words, the Scofield Bible equates the

2. *The New Scofield Reference Bible* (New York: Oxford University Press, 1967), p. 1163.

baptism of the Spirit in the Gospels to the filling
of the Spirit in Acts 2:4, and Acts 2:4 describes what
happens to believers when they are saved—they are
added to the body of Christ. By the way, the word
"filling" in Acts 2:4 and in Ephesians 5:18 is a
translation of two different Greek words. Thus, the
experiences these verses describe are two different
experiences. The one experience involved the disciples
and early converts (Acts 2), believing Samaritans
(Acts 8), believing Gentiles (Acts 10), and everyone
who has believed in Jesus Christ from that day to this.

This, in my opinion, is what the "baptism of the
Spirit" refers to in the Bible—not a "second blessing"
subsequent to salvation. Commenting on the second
chapter of Acts, the Day of Pentecost chapter, *The
Pulpit Commentary* says, "Accept the Lord Jesus
Christ as your Teacher, Lord, Saviour; be baptized into
Him."[3] With many others, *The Pulpit Commentary*
connects the baptism with salvation.

*The baptism of the Spirit which it was our Lord's
prerogative to bestow was, strictly speaking,
something that took place once for all on the Day of
Pentecost when He poured forth 'the promise of the
Father' on His disciples and thus constituted them the
new people of God.*[4]

Thus, Dr. F. F. Bruce too equates Spirit baptism with
the Spirit's putting the early believers into the body of
Christ for the first time. This does not mean that
there may not be another work of grace bestowed by

3. *The Pulpit Commentary* (Grand Rapids, Mich.: Eerdmans, 1950), Vol.
18, p. 62.
4. Bruce, F. F., *Commentary on the Book of Acts, The New International
Commentary on the New Testament* (Grand Rapids, Mich.: Eerdmans,
1964), p. 76.

the indwelling Spirit after salvation, but only that most scholars feel that the expression "baptism in the Spirit" should not be used to describe such an additional experience.

As long as people know what they really mean when they use "baptism" to describe what the Bible generally calls "filling," we should not quibble with them; the disagreement is about vocabulary, not experience. At the same time, when some of us use other words to describe what our charismatic friends choose to call "baptism," they should be careful that they do not write us off as if we knew nothing about the Holy Spirit simply because we do not use the words they like. Let's not lose fellowship over semantics.

Frankly, the charismatic interpretation may be valid (though I feel they misapply the terms). As long as they understand what they mean and give the rest of us the option of using different expressions, which we feel are more accurate scripturally, I do not feel that we should cut ourselves off from each other. Different vocabulary is not sufficient reason for broken fellowship.

When I talk about our experiences with the Holy Spirit in the chapters which follow, I will usually use expressions such as "filled with the Spirit," "receiving the Spirit," "yielding to the Spirit," etc. If I should use any form of the word "baptism," I will be doing so out of consideration for my charismatic friends. In other words, I expect to use the words "baptism" and "filling" synonymously—not because I see them as synonymous, but because I want charismatics and noncharismatics to benefit from this book.

It is quite evident from Christian history that many of us come into a new experience with God after we are saved—sometimes long afterwards. Therefore, we *do* experience a "second blessing," stemming from a crisis experience.

Perhaps it would be helpful at this point to give a brief history of the charismatic movement, a history with many triumphs and many falls. What church or denomination hasn't had the same?

As most people know, the charismatic movement grew out of Pentecostal doctrine, which became relatively widespread after the turn of the century. Though it did exist before that time, the big boom of Pentecostalism has been in the twentieth century.

I have no doubt that a good scholar could give dates, name names, and thoroughly document what I am going to base on my own observation over a period of more than thirty-five years in the ministry, a ministry that has included just about every evangelical group there is. My fellowship with God's people has taken me into most of the world. This gives me a rather broad basis from which to speak about matters that I did not learn out of a book but from the people who hold them dear.

Perhaps the first branch to grow from the Pentecostal tree involved several groups that chose to drop the word "Pentecostal" and rather refer to themselves as "Full Gospel" or some similar name. They remained substantially Pentecostal doctrinally, but tried to allow room for those who had not been blessed with any of the more dramatic gifts— particularly tongues and healing. However, practically speaking one could not see much difference between these groups and the traditional Pentecostal churches. Basically, the only thing that really changed was the vocabulary. Spirit baptism, tongues, and healing were still their major thrusts. However, they did have a "softer sell" on the dramatic gifts as a necessary evidence of the baptism.

The next step was to open the door for members of other denominations—including Roman Catholics —to share their charismatic experiences. Full Gospel breakfasts and dinners, led largely by men in the Christian Business Men Committee tradition, emphasized testimonies by people who did not have a Pentecostal or Full Gospel denominational label but who would say they were Baptists, Presbyterians, or some other mainline church member—but who had received the baptism. Now there was a deliberate attempt to avoid the term "Pentecostal," although there was little difference between the two.

Pentecostals still maintained that speaking in tongues was necessary, as they always had. The broader group said it was not necesssary, yet often acted as if it were.

The most recent move, still in its infancy, has been to widen the umbrella to include anybody who has received the baptism. The new—but really old—word that was coined to describe these people was "charismatic." It would seem that it is important to charismatic believers that they stay in their original churches, and to date (1977) they have not formed a charismatic denomination as such.

As usual when a new movement spreads rapidly and worldwide, some Christians tend to take rather extreme positions in their opinions about it. To me, it is unfair to casually or carelessly dismiss such a large group of obviously sincere and godly people. It would be a show of gross stupidity or unbelievable ignorance to refuse to admit the impact that this group has made around the world.

I know personally a number of people whose lives

have dramatically changed as a result of the efforts of people involved in the charismatic movement. This would have to include several of the celebrities, athletes, and politicians who now profess Christ. Although he is predominantly a Southern Baptist, it would be difficult to miss the effect on the life of U. S. President Jimmy Carter by his evangelist sister, who has most of the trappings of a charismatic.

If you are involved in world missions, you are certainly aware of the incredible impact of charismatics in some areas of the world, perhaps most notably in the countries of South America, where charismatics probably have a larger following than all the other church groups combined. In the Scandinavian countries it would be fair to say that by far the majority of evangelicals are Pentecostal (Scandinavians are not afraid of the word).

Despite the fact that some charismatics' extreme practices leave me cold and uncomfortable at best, charismatics have introduced a warmth, a love, and a vitality into many churches where the services had begun to resemble a funeral rather than worship of the living God.

On the other hand, I don't think God expects us to see the assets of our charismatic brethren but remain blind to some of the problems that a few (I repeat, a few) charismatics have created. Unfortunately, a few people in any group can spoil the reputation of all the rest, and this may be one of the dangers that charismatic Christians will have to face bravely and deal with.

Most charismatics are quite emphatic in declaring that speaking in tongues is not the most important gift, and that it is certainly not the only necessary evidence of the baptism. However, I have talked with some whose testimonies seem to contradict their doctrine. They *do* covet the gift of tongues and they *do* lean very heavily in the direction of faith healing in a demanding sort of way. Furthermore, one cannot talk to this sort of charismatic for long without coming to the conclusion that they feel you are a sort of second-class Christian if you do not talk freely (with their vocabulary) about the baptism, healing, and tongues. I heard one person express it this way: "Tongues is not necessary, but it is the icing on the cake."

Now, I have no objection to someone believing this, but honesty should lead such a person to call himself by the proper name. He is (doctrinally, though not necessarily denominationally) Pentecostal. Why be ashamed of it or deny it?

There are also a few charismatics who preach the baptism much more forcefully and more often than they preach the gospel. To put it into baseball language, it would seem to me that they think you can get to second base without touching first. For instance, a Roman Catholic can continue to observe the mass, go to confession, pray through the saints, pray to the Virgin, and accept the infallibility of the Pope and of Roman Catholic church tradition and yet receive the baptism. It would seem to me that the most important thing in conversing with Catholics would be to concentrate on those great issues for which Martin Luther nearly died—that justification comes by faith through grace, and that Christianity starts when a person trusts Christ and only Christ as his Savior without reliance on works of any kind. Surely this is the "first blessing" and must come before any "second blessing."

I heard one of the best known of the converted

movie stars give his testimony. In the audience were a great many unsaved people, but never once did he mention the fact that he had been saved, that he had accepted Christ. The whole story centered around the baptism and the miracles that followed. I have no doubt that the man had really been born again, but the unsaved guests in the audience weren't told about that and certainly would not have learned from that testimony that it is necessary to accept Jesus Christ as your Savior before you can become a child of God—and that the Holy Spirit will do nothing for you until you are his temple and he dwells in you.

A few charismatics are quick to put their label on any, if not all, of the great Christian leaders of the past—particularly if they wrote about any kind of an experience with the Holy Spirit. For example, Rev. Charles G. Finney preached Christ from about 1821 through 1868, long before the Pentecostal movement got under way and at a time when the issue of speaking in tongues was rarely discussed. However, Finney often talked about the baptism of the Spirit and described his conversion and baptism experiences in very vivid language:

But as I turned and was about to take a seat by the fire, I received a mighty baptism of the Holy Ghost. Without any expectation of it, without ever having the thought in my mind that there was any such thing for me, without any recollection that I had ever heard the thing mentioned by any person in the world, the Holy Spirit descended upon me in a manner that seemed to go through me, body and soul. I could feel the impression like a wave of electricity going through and through me. Indeed, it seemed to come in waves and waves of liquid love; for I

*could not express it in any other way. It seemed like
the very breath of God. I can recollect distinctly
that it seemed to fan me, like immense wings.*

*. . . I wept aloud with joy and love; and I do not
know but I should say, I literally bellowed out the
unutterable gushings of my heart.* [5]

This is the kind of paragraph that should delight
any Christian and stir his heart, but it would be unfair
to conclude from this testimony that Finney was
charismatic in the modern sense of the term or that he
spoke in tongues. He makes it clear that he was
not seeking this experience, nor did he expect it;
and he says nothing whatever about any dramatic
demonstration that followed. Furthermore, it
happened almost immediately after his conversion
with no appreciable time lapse whatever.

A few of the more enthusiastic adherents of the
baptism, tongues, and healing also have a tendency to
denounce their own noncharismatic churches
because, according to them, they never preach about
the Holy Spirit. Though not always, this criticism is
often unfair. What the critics really mean is that
their churches do not use the same vocabulary they
do and do not encourage the same physical and vocal
demonstrations. To be more fair, these folk should
admit that many churches existing before the modern
charismatic movement and even before the
Pentecostal movement greatly emphasized the
ministry of the Spirit, though they didn't use the
charismatic terminology.

For example, at the Finney revivals the Holy Spirit
was central, but tongues were seldom if ever

5. Finney, Charles G., *Memoirs* (New York: Fleming H. Revell Company,
1876), p. 20.

mentioned. And, English Keswick has as its sole purpose to teach Christian people about the Holy Spirit; in excess of 5,000 people have met annually since 1875 in the English lake district to listen to some of God's choicest Bible teachers talk about the Holy Spirit. The vocabulary they use would be "the Spirit-filled life," "the victorious life," "the abundant life." Strictly speaking, they are not charismatic, because they talk more about the fruit of the Spirit than about the dramatic gifts of the Spirit.

Keswick, of course, is no longer limited to England. Almost every English-speaking country in the world now has its own Keswick conference, and there are others in many of the non-English-speaking countries. It has been my privilege to participate in a number of these all over the world. None of them is "charismatic," but all of them gather around the Holy Spirit.

The Christian and Missionary Alliance is a newer denomination that has always majored on the work of the Holy Spirit, much along the same lines as the Keswick conferences. For the most part Alliance churches are not charismatic as such. Even their emphasis on healing is quite different. Their doctrine connects healing with the atonement and not so much as a special gift of the Spirit, although they have had "healers."

All of the Holiness groups—Salvation Army, Nazarene, Free Methodist, Covenant, etc.—have emphasized the ministry of the Holy Spirit, but they do not speak in tongues and the dramatic gifts are not emphasized. They are not charismatic, but they are certainly Holy Ghost conscious.

The Peoples Church has sometimes been accused of being silent about the Holy Spirit. On one occasion

I took out my record book and showed one of our
young people exactly how many times I had preached
on the Holy Spirit that year, in addition to all the
comments made about the Holy Spirit when speaking
on other topics—plus messages about the Holy Spirit
that had been preached by many of our guest
preachers. In our Sunday school classes our teachers
had also covered the subject of the Holy Spirit. That
was all in one year.

We maintain a rather extensive bookstand in our
main lobby, and at any given time a large number of
the books will center around some aspect of the
deeper life. My father, the founder of The Peoples
Church, has always preached the Keswick-Alliance
deeper life message and has always had at least one or
two of his own books on the subject available.

Obviously this young person had been influenced by
some local charismatic Christian that had convinced
him that because we don't use the charismatic
vocabulary, we know nothing about the Holy Spirit
and have not had any experience with him. Again
I say, Let's not lose fellowship over semantics.

In the following chapters, we will look at all the
Bible passages dealing with tongues. Whether you
consider yourself Pentecostal, charismatic,
noncharismatic, or whatever, please read on. Whether
or not you agree with the interpretations I feel most
biblical, please look over the material carefully.
Above all, remember that regardless of whether or not
we share the same views on the gifts of the Spirit, I
want your fellowship in Christ. More specifically,
I need your fellowship, and you need mine.

Again, I am not zeroing in on tongues because I feel
this is the central issue, but rather because I feel it is
a typical issue and, frankly, because a few charismatics

so overemphasize this particular gift that I feel a response is needed.

Again, whatever I have said that could be considered critical has not been addressed to the great majority of my charismatic friends. But I am confronted continually by a minority who should receive some censure from the main group for the reasons I have mentioned. Many of those in the charismatic movement do not promote tongues excessively, do not look down on their noncharismatic friends, and admit that the charismatic movement does not have a corner on the ministry of the Holy Spirit. I appreciate their openness and flexibility.

Above all, while we should all be true to the Word of God in these matters as we feel that the Holy Spirit is guiding us, we should not allow this kind of disagreement to rob us of fellowship. We are children of God and brothers and sisters in Christ, not because we talk about the "baptism" rather than the "filling" of the Spirit, nor because we speak in tongues or do not speak in tongues. We are members of God's family because we have been justified by faith through our Lord Jesus Christ by the grace of God. In him we are one.

CHAPTER SIX
WHAT DOES
THE BIBLE SAY
ABOUT TONGUES?

Eight passages in the Bible mention the gift of tongues. One is in the Old Testament, one in the Gospel of Mark, three in the book of Acts, and three in 1 Corinthians. Tongues is a scriptural gift—we cannot condemn all manifestations of it as the work of the devil or mere demonstrations of the flesh.

It is also true that most of the New Testament books do not discuss tongues at all. Neither Matthew, Luke, John, the other Pauline epistles, Hebrews, James, Peter, John, Jude, nor Revelation say a word about it. For this reason, as well as others that will be discussed fully in another chapter, it is dangerous to conclude that those who do not speak in tongues have never experienced the baptism of the Holy Ghost and are much less spiritually than they should be.

THE OLD TESTAMENT

"For with stammering lips and another tongue will he speak to this people" (Isaiah 28:11).

There are two interpretations of this Old Testament passage. Some see it as a clear prophecy of Pentecost and the gift of tongues. Others feel that it is a prophecy of doom to Samaria and Jerusalem. Both had heard the Word of God, "precept upon precept; line upon line," but they had stubbornly refused to obey it. Finally God warned them that they would be conquered and ruled by barbarians who would give them orders in a foreign language, or at best in the Hebrew tongue but spoken in a stammering manner and with a foreign accent.

There is also a passage in Joel that does not specifically mention tongues, but the New Testament affirms that it is a prophecy of the Pentecostal experience described in the second chapter of Acts: "And it shall come to pass afterward, that I will pour out my Spirit upon all flesh; and your sons and your daughters shall prophesy, your old men shall dream dreams, your young men shall see visions: And also upon the servants and upon the handmaids in those days will I pour out my Spirit" (Joel 2:28, 29). The Apostle Peter explained to the crowd on the Day of Pentecost, "This is that which was spoken by the prophet Joel" (Acts 2:16).

THE BOOK OF MARK

If you delete the last seven verses of Mark because they do not appear in the more ancient manuscripts, there would be absolutely no reference to the gift of tongues anywhere in the four Gospels. However, the Holy Spirit has permitted us to include these verses in our canon of Scriptures for a very long time; and because they are in complete harmony with the rest of the New Testament, many accept them at equal value.

"And these signs shall follow them that believe; in my name shall they cast out devils; they shall speak with new tongues; they shall take up serpents; and if they drink any deadly thing, it shall not hurt them; they shall lay hands on the sick, and they shall recover" (Mark 16:17, 18).

This is a prophecy of the risen Lord and he declares that five signs will follow those who believe. Four of these were fulfilled early enough to be recorded elsewhere in the Bible.

The sick were healed and devils were cast out: "There came also a multitude out of the cities round about unto Jerusalem, bringing sick folks, and them which were vexed with unclean spirits: and they were healed every one" (Acts 5:16).

Paul was bitten by a serpent and it did not hurt him. "And when Paul had gathered a bundle of sticks, and laid them on the fire, there came a viper out of the heat, and fastened on his hand. . . . And he shook off the beast into the fire, and felt no harm" (Acts 28:3, 5).

The first instance of tongues is recorded in the second chapter of Acts.

There is no account in the Bible of anyone drinking poison without ill effects, but the early Church Fathers mention it. In the fourth and fifth centuries Eusebius attributed this experience to Justus Barsabas, and Augustine related the same miraculous deliverance of John.

Four things stand out in these verses:

(1) The gift of tongues is associated with salvation, not with a later experience with the Holy Spirit. The concept of a second spiritual experience subsequent to salvation does not appear until the book of Acts.

(2) There is no mention here of duration. Jesus does not say that these gifts will continue throughout the church age, nor does he say that they will cease after the apostolic age.

(3) Five gifts are listed and none is given precedence over the others.

(4) On the basis of these verses, if we feel that the gift of tongues is a necessity for every Christian,

then we must conclude that the other signs are equally essential.

ACTS 2:1-11

The second chapter of Acts tells the remarkable story of the Day of Pentecost when the gift of tongues was received and used by the Apostles for the first time.

"And when the day of Pentecost was fully come, they were all with one accord in one place. And suddenly there came a sound from heaven as of a rushing mighty wind, and it filled all the house where they were sitting. And there appeared unto them cloven tongues like as of fire, and it sat upon each of them. And they were all filled with the Holy Ghost, and began to speak with other tongues, as the Spirit gave them utterance. And there were dwelling at Jerusalem Jews, devout men, out of every nation under heaven. Now when this was noised abroad, the multitude came together, and were confounded, because that every man heard them speak in his own language. And they were all amazed and marveled, saying one to another, Behold, are not all these which speak Galileans? And how hear we every man in our own tongue, wherein we were born? Parthians, and Medes, and Elamites, and the dwellers in Mesopotamia, and in Judea, and Cappadocia, in Pontus and Asia, Phrygia, and Pamphylia, in Egypt, and in the parts of Libya about Cyrene, and strangers of Rome, Jews and proselytes, Cretes and Arabians, we do hear them speak in our tongues the wonderful works of God."

We can make the following observations:

(1) There was a very definite purpose for tongues at this time. The apostles were able to preach the

gospel to a large number of people from many parts of the world—and each heard it in his own language, without a Galilean accent. Some commentators think that the disciples spoke in their own language or in an ecstatic nonhuman tongue, and the sound came to the ears of the hearers in their language. This would mean that the miracle took place in the hearing, not in the speaking.

The entire context of the story has led the majority of scholars to affirm, however, that the disciples were actually enabled to speak in a tongue that was foreign to them but familiar to people in the crowd. In either case, the miracle made it possible to reach many people in a short time with the gospel message.

(2) There is no record in the Bible that this particular use of the gift of tongues was ever repeated. In the Scriptures, this aspect of tongues is peculiar to the Day of Pentecost. Although there may be isolated instances when a person has miraculously spoken a foreign language in order to reach someone with the gospel, it would seem that this use of tongues is not prominent today. If it were, missionaries would not have to learn a foreign language when they go to the field. But even the missionaries of the Full Gospel churches have to spend months in language study.

(3) The tongues experience in this case did not involve an interpreter—nor did it in any other instance that is recorded in the book of Acts. It may be that the gift of interpretation was added by the Holy Spirit before Paul wrote his first epistle to the Corinthians. This fact would support the Pentecostal concept that tongues as an evidence and tongues as a gift are distinct from each other. The first does not require interpretation; the second does.

(4) In this instance, being "filled with the Holy

Ghost" came after and was separate from salvation. It would be pressing the point a bit too much to conclude that those in the upper room had not already been saved. But it would be in line with the traditional commentators, some of whom have been quoted earlier, to conclude that these "saved" people became the church for the first time at Pentecost and that the "baptism of the Spirit" added them to the body of Christ.

ACTS 10:44-48

"They of the circumcision which believed were astonished, as many as came with Peter, because that on the Gentiles also was poured out the gift of the Holy Ghost. For they heard them speak with tongues, and magnify God" (vv. 45, 46).

The second chapter of Acts tells the story of the Jewish Pentecost, and the tenth chapter records the Gentile Pentecost. The major point of this rather long passage about Peter and Cornelius is that salvation and the infilling of the Holy Spirit was for Gentiles as well as Jews. Peter was not really convinced until he saw the same thing happen to these people as had happened to him and the other disciples in the upper room—they received the Holy Spirit and spoke in tongues.

There are one or two differences between the stories in Acts 2 and 10:

(1) Cornelius and his group had this experience simultaneously with their salvation. Peter was preaching the gospel—and the instant they believed, they were saved, filled with the Spirit, and spoke in tongues.

(2) Water baptism followed the whole transaction—

one of the best evidences that water baptism is a witness to salvation, not a part of it. These people were not only saved but also filled with the Holy Spirit before they were baptized.

No one could deny that in this chapter, speaking in tongues is accepted by Peter as conclusive evidence that Cornelius and his friends had indeed received the Holy Spirit.

ACTS 19:1-6

"And when Paul had laid his hands upon them, the Holy Ghost came on them; and they spake with tongues, and prophesied" (v. 6).

Apollos had preached in Ephesus and at least twelve men had been convinced that Jesus was the Christ. They had believed and had been baptized in the manner of John the Baptist. Apparently Apollos had left Jerusalem before the Day of Pentecost and knew nothing about the advent of the Holy Ghost. His converts were accepted as disciples because of their faith in Christ, but they professed to Paul, "We have not so much as heard whether there be any Holy Ghost."

Paul rebaptized them in the name of Jesus Christ. He laid his hands on them and they received the Holy Spirit. The immediate result was that they spoke in tongues and prophesied.

CONCLUSIONS FROM THESE PASSAGES

(1) Jesus said five signs would follow them that believe. He did not give precedence to any one (Mark 16).

(2) The initial Pentecost was to facilitate preaching the gospel to many people at the same time, and this

aspect of the gift was never repeated again in the Bible (Acts 2).

(3) The Pentecostal experience agreed with our Lord's ascension message when he singled out a major ministry of the Holy Spirit—to empower his people to be witnesses to the world (Acts 1:8).

(4) The filling of the Holy Spirit may occur at the time of salvation or subsequent to it (Acts 2, 10).

(5) In one of these five passages, the gift of tongues alone is accepted as evidence of the reception of the Holy Spirit (Acts 10).

(6) In one passage tongues and prophesying are linked equally as evidences (Acts 19).

(7) There is no indication in any of these five passages that tongues or any of these gifts was to cease after the apostles were gone.

(8) Vibrating throughout the New Testament is the message that Christianity involves an experience with the Holy Spirit.

CHAPTER SEVEN
FIRST CORINTHIANS TWELVE

Not everyone who speaks in tongues received that gift from God. In fact, speaking in tongues may be induced by the devil or by the Holy Spirit.

Also, the Holy Spirit does not seem to give all the gifts to any one person, and no one gift is necessarily given to all believers.

These are the broad concepts of 1 Corinthians 12, written to a church that had misused the gift of tongues by elevating it to an unwarranted position of prominence. It is important to notice that Paul does not forbid tongues, nor does he make it any less important than the other gifts. He simply puts it back in its God-given place. We need his balanced view today.

The passage breaks easily into four general divisions, enabling us to grasp and remember its contents.

VERSES 1-3

"Now concerning spiritual gifts, brethren, I would not have you ignorant. Ye know that ye were Gentiles, carried away unto these dumb idols, even as ye were led. Wherefore I give you to understand, that no man speaking by the Spirit of God calleth Jesus accursed: and that no man can say that Jesus is the Lord, but by the Holy Ghost."

Apparently the Corinthian Christians had heard a great many people speaking in tongues. Some of the messages were good and proclaimed Jesus Christ as Lord. Others were quite alarming because they

cursed the Lord. Whether the Corinthians had actually
written the apostle and asked for an answer, or
whether word had come to him in some other way, we
do not know. At any rate, he included this chapter
and the next two in his epistle to elaborate on the
validity, the prominence, and the use of tongues in the
church.

He blamed the Corinthians' spiritual ignorance on
the fact that they had been converted from heathenism
and therefore did not have the long tradition of
the Jewish faith and Scriptures behind them. Pagans
allowed their idol gods to do many strange things, and
it was not inconceivable for them to contradict
themselves. Paul makes it clear in these three verses
that the Holy Spirit never contradicts himself. A
good general rule is this: If the ecstatic utterance
glorifies Jesus as Lord, it is certainly not the work of
the devil. If it pronounces a curse on Jesus, it cannot be
the work of the Holy Spirit. Paul adds other guidelines
for the use of this gift in chapter 14, but he starts
here with this one broad foundation principle.

All tongues activity is not the work of the Holy
Spirit, but it is not all the work of the devil either.
Spiritual people should be able to distinguish between
the two. "Beloved, believe not every spirit, but try the
spirits whether they are of God: because many false
prophets are gone out into the world" (1 John 4:1).

It is dangerous to condemn all speaking in tongues
as being of the devil. It is equally dangerous to
accept all manifestations of tongues indiscriminately.
Both positions are untenable from a scriptural
standpoint. It is a well attested fact that even outside
the Christian community, among members of other
religions, there are many examples of the tongues
phenomenon—or certainly something akin to it.

VERSES 4-11

"Now there are diversities of gifts, but the same Spirit. And there are differences of administrations, but the same Lord. And there are diversities of operations, but it is the same God which worketh all in all. But the manifestation of the Spirit is given to every man to profit withal. For to one is given by the Spirit the word of wisdom; to another the word of knowledge by the same Spirit; to another faith by the same Spirit; to another the gifts of healing by the same Spirit; to another the working of miracles; to another prophecy; to another discerning of spirits; to another divers kinds of tongues; to another the interpretation of tongues: But all these worketh that one and the selfsame Spirit, dividing to every man severally as he will."

The apostle lists nine gifts of the Spirit. There is probably no significance in the order in which he names them. Maybe he put tongues and interpretation last because the Corinthians had so consistently put them first. This is not to say that they are any less important, but perhaps to point out that the other gifts are just as important.

(1) *Wisdom* was the ability to make spiritual decisions before the New Testament was completed and the special ability to properly interpret the Bible after it was available.

(2) *Knowledge* has to do with the ability to accumulate and retain spiritual truth, and probably involves the capacity to study.

(3) *Faith* here is the ability to perform miracles, and is not the same as the faith that brought salvation to all Christians.

(4) *Healing* is a special kind of miracle and involves a separate gift. The use of the plural "gifts" in this case

might indicate a slightly different gift for different diseases.

(5) *Miracles* would be more accurately translated "powers" and is not so much concerned with wonder-working as with the special ability of some Christians to perform tasks requiring more than human strength. This might include the stamina of the martyrs in the face of torture and death, or the sheer endurance of early Christians throughout a long and difficult ministry.

(6) *Prophecy* is not generally related to pronouncements about the future, as was the case in the Old Testament. It is more concerned with special revelations of the Lord to his church about what to believe and how to act.

(7) *Discerning of spirits* is the ability (implied in the first three verses) to know what is of God and what is of the devil.

(8) *Tongues* is an utterance of the human tongue that is produced by the Holy Spirit. It has several uses. Once, as we have seen, it was given to enable the disciples to preach in a foreign language (Acts 2). Once it was accepted as the sole evidence that the Holy Spirit had been received (Acts 10). Once it was one of two evidences (Acts 19). Jesus said it would be one of five evidences of salvation (Mark 16). Sometimes it is for the personal edification of the believer (1 Corinthians 14:4), and sometimes it is a means of edifying the whole church (1 Corinthians 14:5).

(9) *Interpretation of tongues* is the ability to translate an utterance that has been given by the Holy Spirit in an unknown tongue into a language known by the hearers. This can be done by the person who spoke in tongues (1 Corinthians 14:5) or by another person (1 Corinthians 14:27).

The thesis of these verses is that it is the same Spirit that distributes at least nine different gifts to different believers.

"the same Spirit." There is absolutely no diversity in the source of spiritual gifts. They all come from the Spirit of God. The words "same Spirit" are repeated four times, and a fifth time Paul emphasizes the same thought with "selfsame." The other two persons of the Trinity are seen in verses 5 and 6 as being in complete agreement in the distribution.

Whatever else we may see in this passage, we must recognize that our gifts come from the Holy Spirit and therefore we can take absolutely no credit for them personally. The healer is no more important than the helper and the preacher no more important than the one who speaks in tongues. It is the Holy Spirit that is important. He imparts the power. He distributes the gifts. He produces the results.

"diversities of gifts." In describing the distribution of the nine gifts, the apostle starts with the expression "to one" and then with each new gift he uses the phrase "to another." That phrase occurs eight times within three verses, obviously to emphasize the diversity of the gifts. Nothing in these verses necessitates that we believe that any one Christian has all nine gifts. Nor do these verses demand that any one of these is given to everybody.

VERSES 12-26

"For as the body is one, and hath many members, and all the members of that one body, being many, are one body: so also is Christ. For by one Spirit are

we all baptized into one body, whether we be Jews or
Gentiles, whether we be bond or free; and have been
all made to drink into one Spirit. For the body is not
one member, but many. If the foot shall say, Because I
am not the hand, I am not of the body; is it therefore
not of the body? And if the ear shall say, Because
I am not the eye, I am not of the body; is it therefore
not of the body? If the whole body were an eye, where
were the hearing? If the whole were hearing, where
were the smelling? But now hath God set the members
every one of them in the body, as it hath pleased
him. And if they were all one member, where were the
body? But now are they many members, yet but one
body. And the eye cannot say unto the hand, I have no
need of thee: nor again the head to the feet, I have
no need of you. Nay, much more those members of
the body, which seem to be more feeble, are necessary:
And those members of the body, which we think
to be less honorable, upon these we bestow more
abundant honor; and our uncomely parts have more
abundant comeliness. For our comely parts have no
need: but God hath tempered the body together,
having given more abundant honor to that part which
lacked: That there should be no schism in the
body; but that the members should have the same care
one for another. And whether one member suffer,
all the members suffer with it; or one member be
honored, all the members rejoice with it."

The church is like a living body. Each person in it
is one of the members. Some are hands, some feet,
some eyes, some ears, etc.

Every member is important. The foot is no less
important than the hand, the ear no less important
than the eye. How foolish it would be if the
whole body were an eye! Then how could it hear? Or if

the whole body were an ear, how could it smell?

The point is that we are not all eyes, ears, hands, or feet. We are "many members, yet but one body." If we were all the same, we would not be a body at all, but some sort of monstrosity.

Once this point of diversity is established, then we are forced to admit that we need each other. The eye needs the hand and the head needs the feet. Even the most insignificant and weakest member is necessary. Sometimes we pay more attention to these members than to those that seem more prominent. Furthermore, this diverse body, the church, is such a complete unity that when one member suffers all suffer, and when one member rejoices all rejoice.

VERSES 27-31

"Now ye are the body of Christ, and members in particular. And God hath set some in the church, first apostles, secondarily prophets, thirdly teachers, after that miracles, then gifts of healings, helps, governments, diversities of tongues. Are all apostles? are all prophets? are all teachers? are all workers of miracles? Have all the gifts of healing? do all speak with tongues? do all interpret? But covet earnestly the best gifts: and yet show I unto you a more excellent way."

Continuing with the same illustration, Paul thinks of the various gifts of the Holy Spirit as having their place in the members of the living body. In the place of hands, feet, eyes, and ears, he puts apostles, prophets, teachers, miracles, healings, helps, governments, and tongues. He had asked the foolish question, "What if the whole body were an eye or an ear?" Now he asks the questions, "Are all apostles?

are all prophets? etc." Each body member is important. Each gift of the Spirit is important.

There can be only one answer to Paul's rhetorical questions—No! Just as the whole body cannot be an eye, so everyone does not have the gift of tongues. This does not mean that one person cannot have more than one gift, or that several persons won't have the same gift. It simply means that no one gift is given to all and no one has all the gifts of the Spirit.

The Corinthians had been putting the gift of tongues above all others. Paul now sets this gift where it belongs—one among many.

He urges these believers to seek the best. Since he has not said which is the best, but rather in his illustration of the body has indicated that all are equally important, we might properly conclude that we should seek for that gift which the Holy Spirit knows is best for us.

It is highly probable that these verses do not present an exhaustive list of the gifts. Nor is it likely that a compilation of all the Bible passages would give us a complete list. I would assume that although the inspired writers indicate a generous number of gifts, they are but examples of many more and the lists are always open-ended.

CHAPTER EIGHT
FIRST CORINTHIANS FOURTEEN

Review: Tongues is quite obviously a gift of the Holy
Spirit, but like any other gift it can be misused and
abused. This seems to have been one of the problems
with the church in Corinth, and Paul wrote
1 Corinthians 12—14 to put tongues back into its
proper place, to show that it is of no value whatever if
not motivated by love, and to say that it will cease
only when the Lord returns.

Perhaps you noticed that we skipped over
1 Corinthians 13, another passage mentioning tongues.
You'll see why when you get to Part Three.

Chapter 14 is a continuation of the same theme, but
now the apostle deals with the relative value of
tongues and prophecy—and the practical problem of
their use in a service of public worship.

VERSES 1-6

Prophecy has a much broader scope than the
interpretation of a message from God given in an
unknown tongue. We cannot read the Old Testament
without realizing that the prophets were not simply
passive voices relaying God's messages to man
without the use of their own personalities, talents,
and intellects. It is much more realistic to think
of the Old Testament prophet as a man who received a
message from God and then used every means at
his disposal to convey that exact message to his
people. Sometimes he taught, sometimes he preached.

On occasion he illustrated the message with stories
or even acted it out dramatically.

The actual meaning of the Greek noun *prophetes*
is "one who speaks for another or one who speaks
beforehand." The preposition *pro* in Greek can
mean "for" or "before."

The Hebrew noun *nabi* means one who announces.
The New Bible Dictionary says that *nabi* can either
mean "one who is called, or one who calls, i.e., to men
in the name of God."[1]

There is no question but that the prophets received
the exact content of their message from God and
sometimes they simply transmitted it. However, I am
inclined to conclude that much of their prophesying
was done in their own words in the form of preaching
or teaching. Obviously each prophet used his own
vocabulary, and some of them used their writing
ability. The written message was considered prophecy,
just as was the spoken. It should always be
remembered that the written Word is completely
inerrant in every area, even though it may have
been presented through the vocabulary and personality
of a certain person.

Each prophet stamped the marks of his own
personality and experience on his word. The books of
Amos and Jeremiah are as different as were the
personalities of the two prophets. We cannot read
either book without being convinced of two things:
These were the words of God and the prophet was
obviously God's mouthpiece, but they were also the
vocabulary of a certain man, at a certain time,
spoken under certain circumstances that were peculiar
to that man. He was not simply a passive voice.

1. Douglas, J. D., *The New Bible Dictionary* (Grand Rapids, Mich.:
Eerdmans, 1962), p. 1037.

As a matter of fact, sometimes the prophecy was acted out. God told Isaiah to go naked and barefoot for three years (Isaiah 20) as an illustration. Jeremiah smashed a potter's vessel (Jeremiah 19).

Nehemiah says the prophets preached (Nehemiah 6:7). John the Baptist is referred to as a prophet because he gave God's message (Luke 7:27, 28). Luke describes Judas and Silas as prophets, but the context of the passage would seem to indicate that they stayed at Antioch and taught the believers over a period of time (Acts 15:32). They were prophets in the sense that they received special revelations from God, and perhaps on occasion they repeated them by rote. It would seem that in this case they taught these revelations until the believers at Antioch understood them. Prophecy may be God's message for a particular time or God's prediction of a future event. Both are prophecy.

Ordinarily this word [prophet] is understood as meaning one who foretells future events. It meant, at the time our English Bible was translated, also a preacher—and prophesying meant preaching.[2]

A great deal of preaching is devoid of any prophetic content. It may be simply a dispensing of religious knowledge. Prophetic preaching would contain a message from God that met the need of the hour. It would be authoritative and infallible—but it might be couched in the words or outline or headings produced by a man's intellect.

The Apostle Paul defines preaching in such a way that he makes it almost synonymous with

2. Cruden, Alexander, *Cruden's Complete Concordance* (Philadelphia: The John C. Winston Company, 1949), p. 517.

prophesying: "that we might know the things that are freely given to us of God. Which things also we speak, not in the words which man's wisdom teacheth, but which the Holy Ghost teacheth" (1 Corinthians 2:12, 13). Paul is defending the "foolishness of preaching" (1 Corinthians 1:21) by saying that his messsage came straight from God (2 Corinthians 4:5).

If we accept prophecy in this wider concept, which would include the inspired preaching or teaching of a message sent from God, then it is not difficult to see why Paul emphasizes it above tongues. Even when it is interpreted, a message in tongues is limited to the original words.

"Follow after charity, and desire spiritual gifts, but rather that ye may prophesy. For he that speaketh in an unknown tongue speaketh not unto men, but unto God: for no man understandeth him; howbeit in the spirit he speaketh mysteries. But he that prophesieth speaketh unto men to edification, and exhortation, and comfort. He that speaketh in an unknown tongue edifieth himself; but he that prophesieth edifieth the church. I would that ye all spake with tongues, but rather that ye prophesied: for greater is he that prophesieth than he that speaketh with tongues, except he interpret, that the church may receive edifying. Now brethren, if I come unto you speaking with tongues, what shall I profit you, except I shall speak to you either by revelation, or by knowledge, or by prophesying, or by doctrine?"

In these first six verses of chapter 14, Paul says that without an interpreter tongues is of little value in a public service, because only God can understand it and therefore the other people are not helped. Prophesying is more valuable because it brings edification, exhortation, and comfort to the entire congregation. These three words constitute a good description of the purposes of preaching.

On the other hand, tongues can be valuable if the message is interpreted. On this condition it would be valuable if all spoke in tongues. Obviously, all did not speak in tongues even in the Corinthian church where they overemphasized it. Verse 5 would indicate that one man might speak in tongues and interpret. In this case he would have both gifts.

VERSES 7-20

"And even things without life giving sound, whether pipe or harp, except they give a distinction in the sounds, how shall it be known what is piped or harped? For if the trumpet give an uncertain sound, who shall prepare himself to the battle? So likewise ye, except ye utter by the tongue words easy to be understood, how shall it be known what is spoken? for ye shall speak into the air. There are, it may be, so many kinds of voices in the world, and none of them is without signification. Therefore if I know not the meaning of the voice, I shall be unto him that speaketh a barbarian, and he that speaketh shall be a barbarian unto me. Even so ye, forasmuch as ye are zealous of spiritual gifts, seek that ye may excel to the edifying of the church.

"Wherefore let him that speaketh in an unknown tongue pray that he may interpret. For if I pray in an unknown tongue, my spirit prayeth, but my understanding is unfruitful. What is it then? I will pray with the spirit, and I will pray with the understanding also: I will sing with the spirit, and I will sing with the understanding also.

"Else, when thou shalt bless with the spirit, how shall he that occupieth the room of the unlearned say Amen at thy giving of thanks, seeing he understandeth not what thou sayest? For thou verily givest thanks well, but the other is not edified.

"I thank my God, I speak with tongues more than ye all: Yet in the church I had rather speak five words with my understanding, that by my voice I might teach others also, than ten thousand words in an unknown tongue. Brethren, be not children in understanding: howbeit in malice be ye children, but in understanding be men."

A good general rule to follow is to seek to do those things in the services that will bless the other members of the church. If we pray or sing, it must be understood by others. If they cannot make sense out of it, they cannot express their agreement by saying "Amen," and they have wasted their time.

Paul testifies to his own ability to speak in tongues, but quickly adds that he would rather speak five words that people could understand than 10,000 words in another tongue. Apparently, the Corinthians had used the Holy Spirit's gift of tongues in a childish manner— simply to bless themselves without consideration of others. The apostle urges them to be mature in their use of this gift, adding that they should be children in malice but men in understanding.

VERSES 21-25

"In the law it is written, With men of other tongues and other lips will I speak unto this people; and yet for all that will they not hear me, saith the Lord. Wherefore tongues are for a sign, not to them that believe, but to them that believe not: but prophesying serveth not for them that believe not, but for them which believe. If therefore the whole church be come together into one place, and all speak with tongues, and there come in those that are unlearned, or unbelievers, will they not say that ye are mad? But if all prophesy, and there come in one that believeth not, or one unlearned, he is convinced of all, he is judged of all: And thus are the secrets of his heart made manifest; and so falling down on his face he will worship God, and report that God is in you of a truth."

This is a complicated passage which on first reading seems to contradict itself. The first verse refers to Isaiah 28:11—"For with stammering lips and another tongue will he speak to this people." It does not say that the gift of tongues is a fulfillment of that prophecy, but that it is a sign to unbelievers just as the foreign tongues of their captors were a sign to the unbelieving Jews.

The next four verses describe the effect speaking in tongues would have on the hardened, stubborn unbeliever as opposed to the man who is not a Christian but is receptive, and therefore a potential believer. The hardened unbeliever would not be turned to God by hearing people speak in tongues. It signifies judgment. But when one who is open, a potential believer—now called unlearned or unbeliever—hears a message in tongues, it will not be a sign to him—it will make him think the speaker is crazy. If the same potential believer—still called "one that believeth not"—hears someone prophesying, he may be convicted of his need and turn to God.

The point to remember here is that the people in question are all non-Christians; but in verse 22 the unbeliever is determined not to believe, and in verses 23, 24 the unbeliever is one who is responsive. Paul is describing how ineffective tongues are among the unsaved. At best they are a sign of judgment to the hardened sinner. At worst they sound like madness to the responsive sinner.

VERSES 26-33

"How is it then, brethren? when ye come together, every one of you hath a psalm, hath a doctrine, hath a tongue, hath a revelation, hath an interpretation. Let all things be done unto edifying. If any man speak in an unknown tongue, let it be by two, or at the most by three, and that by course; and let one interpret. But if there be no interpreter, let him keep silence in the church; and let him speak to himself, and to God. Let the prophets speak two or three, and let the other judge. If any thing be revealed to another that sitteth by, let the first hold his peace. For ye may all prophesy one by one, that all may learn, and all may be comforted. And the spirits of the prophets are subject to the prophets. For God is not the author of confusion, but of peace, as in all churches of the saints."

The gifts of tongues and prophesying are to be used in the church, but at all times two basic principles must be observed: (1) Everything that is done in any public meeting must result in the edification of everyone present, and (2) proper order must be observed at all times.

The early Christians depended upon the leadership of the Holy Spirit in their meetings, and in most cases the gatherings were small enough so that many of those attending were able to take part. Some could sing, others could explain a doctrine, a few were able to speak in tongues, there were those who could pass on revelations, and usually one or two could interpret tongues. Undoubtedly this is but a partial list, because some of the gifts are left out entirely. However, it gives us sufficient information to know how they conducted their services.

Paul emphasizes the importance of concentrating upon those gifts that would edify the believers. Spiritual exercises that bring nothing but personal blessing have no place in a public meeting.

Scripturally, if the gift of tongues is to be used, there must also be interpretation. Furthermore, if the gift is to edify there must be only one person talking at a time, and in any one meeting no more than three messages in tongues should be given.

This means, of course, that the gift of tongues can be controlled. The person who has it can speak or refrain from speaking. Otherwise these rules could not be followed.

The same is true of prophesying: There should be no more than three messages given by the prophets. They do not need interpretation, but they should stand up to the judgment of the other prophets. This would be based on their mutual knowledge and understanding of the Christian faith. A prophet who said anything contrary to the Scriptures or the teaching of the apostles would be publicly corrected. Again, the prophets can control their gift. They can speak or not speak, depending on the progress and order of the service. "God is not the author of confusion, but of peace."

VERSES 34, 35

"Let your women keep silence in the churches: for it is not permitted unto them to speak; but they are commanded to be under obedience, as also saith the law. And if they will learn any thing, let them ask their

husbands at home: for it is a shame for women to
speak in the church."

These verses are not saying that women should
never minister in the church. One basic rule of Bible
interpretation is that Scripture never contradicts itself,
and other passages throughout the Bible give a definite
place to the ministry of women. Joel predicted that
"your sons and your daughters shall prophesy" (2:28),
and Peter declared that the Day of Pentecost was the
fulfillment of this (Acts 2:16). Philip, the evangelist of
Caesarea, had four daughters who prophesied (Acts
21:9). The Apostle Paul gives rather elaborate
instructions about women's head coverings when they
pray or prophesy (1 Corinthians 11:3-16).

Perhaps verse 34 means that women should not talk
to each other or ask their husbands questions during a
service. It is reasonable to conclude that these
Corinthian Christians came directly out of
heathenism, and in a culture where very few women
were literate it is probable that they would have
difficulty understanding what was being said. What
follows seems to indicate this because they are
told to save their questions until they get home.

Or it may simply mean that women should not take
a leading part in any major service of the church,
though they can prophesy and pray in the smaller
gatherings.

VERSES 36-40

"What! came the word of God out from you? or came
it unto you only? If any man think himself to be
a prophet, or spiritual, let him acknowledge that the
things that I write unto you are the commandments of
the Lord. But if any man be ignorant, let him be

ignorant. Wherefore, brethren, covet to prophesy, and forbid not to speak with tongues. Let all things be done decently and in order."

Paul starts these concluding verses with some rather caustic questions, his way of saying: "You did not invent the gospel or the church. It was brought to you. Therefore you are not the final authority on how things should be conducted." If they really possessed the gifts of tongues or prophecy, they would know that what he is saying is true to the apostolic faith.

Verse 38 could be paraphrased, "But if any man does not recognize these rules, he should not be recognized in the meeting." Again we see that although gifts are given by the Holy Spirit, man has some control over their use in public worship.

In conclusion he gives a positive command regarding prophesying and a reminder that tongues should not be forbidden—as long as the rules of decency and order as explained above are observed.

CONCLUSION

It was not the gift of tongues that caused trouble in the church at Corinth. Tongues is an invaluable gift of the Holy Spirit and can never be despised without doing violence to the Word of God. The problem that necessitated these three chapters was an overemphasis of one gift and its misuse in the church.

Sometimes today people will say, "The gift of tongues always causes division and trouble." This is not true, but an overemphasis on this one gift and in some cases a flagrant disregard for the rules that govern it have caused no end of problems and many divisions.

In typical human fashion we tend toward two

extremes. Some are so desperately afraid of the wildfire that they have no fire at all. A complete yielding to the Holy Spirit frightens them and they mention his name only when they pronounce the benediction. These dear folk usually end up as dried up Bible scholars who have all the answers neatly tied up in little bundles, but no power, no warmth, no enthusiasm, and no results.

Others throw the discipline of Scripture to the winds and tumble head over heels in the direction of the dramatic gifts. And these dear ones slide into a highly emotional form of worship that caters to the flesh and results in confusion.

Paul marks out the pathway somewhere between these extremes: use the dramatic gifts but do it decently and in order.

CHAPTER NINE
IS TONGUES THE EVIDENCE OF THE INFILLING OF THE SPIRIT?

There are many passages in the Bible which tell the story of people who received or were filled with the Holy Spirit. I have chosen the eighteen major accounts to see what emphasis the inspired writers put on speaking in tongues. The first six are prophecies about the coming of the Holy Spirit. The next five are incidents which occurred before Pentecost. The twelfth describes the Day of Pentecost itself, and the last six occurred after Pentecost.

(1) JOEL 2:28, 29
"And it shall come to pass afterward, that I will pour out my Spirit upon all flesh; and your sons and your daughters shall prophesy, your old men shall dream dreams, your young men shall see visions: And also upon the servants and upon the handmaids in those days will I pour out my Spirit."

Peter tells us that this is an actual prophecy of what happened at Pentecost. Joel predicts the outpouring of the Holy Spirit and he names some of the signs which would follow—prophecy, dreams, and visions. No mention is made of speaking in tongues.

(2) MATTHEW 3:11 (3) MARK 1:18 (4) LUKE 3:16, 17
(5) JOHN 1:33
"John answered, saying unto them all, I indeed baptize you with water; but one mightier than I cometh,

the latchet of whose shoes I am not worthy to unloose: he shall baptize you with the Holy Ghost and with fire: Whose fan is in his hand, and he will thoroughly purge his floor, and will gather the wheat into his garner; but the chaff he will burn with fire unquenchable" (Luke 3:16, 17).

This story is told by each of the Gospel writers and although these are all accounts of exactly the same event, they were written by four different men under the inspiration of the Holy Spirit. I have chosen Luke's account simply because he was also the author of the book of Acts and obviously cognizant of the events during and following Pentecost. However, the Beloved Physician says nothing about any of the gifts of the Spirit when he tells the story of John's preaching.

He makes it clear that John the Baptist emphasized two other results: (1) The Holy Spirit in the life of the believer would be like fire with its power to purge. Whatever dramatic signs may or may not accompany the coming of the Spirit of God, this cleansing is basic. The person who is not willing to have his life purged by the fire of the Holy Ghost is not ready to be saved or filled with the Spirit.

(2) The advent of the Holy Spirit would be directly associated with the evangelization of the world. John's preaching apparently gave little time to dramatic signs, but there was a strong emphasis on the fact that some people would reject and be burned like chaff.

John the Baptist's prophecy of the baptism of the Holy Spirit makes no mention of speaking in tongues and each of the other three Gospel writers agrees with Luke on this account.

(6) ACTS 1:8
"But ye shall receive power, after that the Holy Ghost

is come upon you: and ye shall be witnesses unto
me both in Jerusalem, and in all Judea, and in Samaria,
and unto the uttermost part of the earth."

This is the prophecy of our Lord. Luke is the human
author of the account, writing under the inspiration of
the Holy Spirit. Jesus emphasizes one immediate
result of the baptism of the Holy Spirit—power to
witness. As in the prophecy of John the Baptist, the
stress is not laid upon miraculous dramatic gifts
but upon the evangelization of the world.

Undoubtedly we will always disagree on some of the
minor points, but let us be firmly agreed on the
fact that the basic purpose of the coming of the Holy
Spirit is to give the people of God power to take
the gospel to the world.

In this account no mention is made of speaking
in tongues.

(7) LUKE 1:41, 42

"And it came to pass, that, when Elisabeth heard the
salutation of Mary, the babe leaped in her womb;
and Elisabeth was filled with the Holy Ghost: And she
spake out with a loud voice, and said, Blessed art
thou among women, and blessed is the fruit of thy
womb."

Elisabeth was filled with the Holy Spirit, and the
result was the revelation to her that Mary was to be
the mother of the Lord. Revelation is one of the gifts
of the Spirit mentioned many times in the later books
of the Bible, but there is no record that Elisabeth spoke
in tongues when she was filled with the Holy Spirit.

(8) LUKE 1:67, 68

"And his father Zacharias was filled with the Holy

Ghost, and prophesied, saying, Blessed be the Lord God of Israel; for he hath visited and redeemed his people."

Zacharias, the father of John the Baptist, was also filled with the Holy Spirit and he immediately received the gift of prophecy, but the Bible does not say he spoke in tongues.

(9) LUKE 2:25, 26

"And, behold, there was a man in Jerusalem, whose name was Simeon; and the same man was just and devout, waiting for the consolation of Israel: and the Holy Ghost was upon him. And it was revealed unto him by the Holy Ghost, that he should not see death, before he had seen the Lord's Christ."

The results when the Holy Spirit came upon Simeon were two-fold—revelation and guidance. It was revealed to him that he would live to see the Christ, and he was led by the Spirit into the temple to see the infant brought in. Revelation is one of the gifts of the Spirit and Simeon received it, but there is no mention of speaking in tongues.

(10) LUKE 4:1, 2

"And Jesus being full of the Holy Ghost returned from Jordan, and was led by the Spirit into the wilderness, being forty days tempted of the devil."

In the case of our Lord, he too was filled with the Spirit and the immediate outcome was a siege of temptation. It is a sobering thought to realize that the results of being filled with the Spirit may not all be pleasant. The devil made a supreme effort to thwart the purpose of God when Jesus was full of the Holy Spirit.

There may be gifts that are exciting or feelings that are overwhelming, but this is certain: the believer who lets the Holy Spirit fill his life will become an immediate target for Satan.

The Son of God came from heaven, but there is no mention in the Bible that he ever used the heavenly tongue—not even when he was "full of the Holy Ghost."

(11) JOHN 20:21-23

"Then Jesus said to them again, Peace be unto you: as my Father hath sent me, even so send I you. And when he had said this, he breathed on them, and saith unto them, Receive ye the Holy Ghost: Whosesoever sins ye remit, they are remitted unto them; and whosesoever sins ye retain, they are retained."

This was one of the postresurrection appearances of the Lord. Whether this is a promise of the Holy Spirit that was to come, or whether the disciples actually received the Holy Spirit when Jesus breathed on them is really not important for our purpose. The point is that whether prophetic or present, receiving the Holy Spirit is connected with the Great Commission, "As my Father hath sent me, even so send I you," and the proclamation of the gospel, "Whosesoever sins ye remit, they are remitted unto them; and whosesoever sins ye retain, they are retained."

Again it is emphasized that the power of the Holy Spirit is given to facilitate the preaching of the gospel. There is no mention of tongues or any other dramatic gift here.

(12) ACTS 2:2-4

"And suddenly there came a sound from heaven as of a rushing mighty wind, and it filled all the house where they were sitting. And there appeared unto them cloven tongues like as of fire, and it sat upon each of them. And they were all filled with the Holy Ghost, and began to speak with other tongues, as the Spirit gave them utterance."

Pentecost was not the first time the Holy Spirit came upon people. All the great battles of the Old Testament characters were waged for God in the power of the Spirit. The Holy Spirit was extremely active during the period recorded in the Gospels. On the Day of Pentecost the difference was that the Holy Spirit came to live and remain in the believer, in the church. Before this he had come and gone, empowering his people for certain special tasks. At Pentecost he came to stay as long as the church was in the world.

There is no doubt that this was a new and very dramatic experience for those involved. Certainly it changed the course of their lives and was the basic impetus of the church from that day on.

There were four dramatic phenomena that took place that day: (1) There was a sound, "as of a rushing mighty wind." (2) There was a sight, "cloven tongues like as of fire." (3) There was a response, "and began to speak with other tongues." And (4) there was a result, "there were added unto them about three thousand souls" (v. 41).

Speaking in tongues is very much in evidence in this passage but so is the sight, the sound, and the result. If we conclude that these verses make speaking in tongues the necessary evidence of the infilling of the Spirit, by exactly the same logic we would have to

say the sound of wind and the tongues of fire were also
a necessary evidence. All three are described and
none is given precedence.

The thrilling part of this story is that the Holy
Spirit came, the gospel was preached, and three
thousand people experienced salvation.

(13) ACTS 4:31

"And when they had prayed, the place was shaken
where they were assembled together; and they were all
filled with the Holy Ghost, and they spake the word
of God with boldness."

For some of these people this may have been a
second filling with the Holy Spirit. For others it may
have been the first. At any rate the evidence that
something had happened to them was that "they spake
the word of God with boldness." There is no mention
here of speaking in tongues.

(14) ACTS 8:14-17

"Now when the apostles which were at Jerusalem
heard that Samaria had received the word of God, they
sent unto them Peter and John: Who, when they
were come down, prayed for them, that they might
receive the Holy Ghost: (For as yet he was fallen upon
none of them: only they were baptized in the name
of the Lord Jesus.) Then laid they their hands on them,
and they received the Holy Ghost."

The evangelist Philip had preached the gospel of
Christ in Samaria and there had been a great response.
Then the church at Jerusalem sent Peter and John
to instruct the believers. When these two had prayed
for the converts and laid hands upon them, those new

Christians received the Holy Spirit.

No mention is made of any dramatic gift having been received on this occasion. Sometimes it is argued that there must have been some sort of evidence that made Simon the sorcerer want to buy the power that came to those receiving the Spirit. This may be true, but the Bible does not say so. Even if it were, there is no reason to conclude that the evidence was tongues rather than prophecy or revelation or healing.

(15) ACTS 9:17-20

"And Ananias went his way, and entered into the house; and putting his hands on him said, Brother Saul, the Lord, even Jesus, that appeared unto thee in the way as thou camest, hath sent me, that thou mightest receive thy sight, and be filled with the Holy Ghost. And immediately there fell from his eyes as it had been scales: and he received sight forthwith, and arose, and was baptized. And when he had received meat, he was strengthened. Then was Saul certain days with the disciples which were at Damascus. And straightway he preached Christ in the synagogues, that he is the Son of God."

We know that the Apostle Paul did speak in tongues (1 Corinthians 14:18), but not a word is said about it as an evidence that he had received the Holy Spirit. Two things are mentioned—that he regained his sight and he began preaching the gospel.

(16) ACTS 10:44-46

"While Peter yet spake these words, the Holy Ghost fell on all them which heard the word. And they of the circumcision which believed were astonished, as many as came with Peter, because that on the Gentiles also was poured out the gift of the Holy Ghost. For they heard them speak with tongues and magnify God."

This is the only passage in the Bible where speaking in tongues stands alone as the evidence of the infilling of the Holy Spirit. There is no doubt about it here. The fact that these Christians from Jerusalem accepted the experience of Cornelius because he spoke in tongues cannot be refuted.

Whether or not we can conclude that this particular case states a general principle is questionable. One of the rules of logic affirms that we should not generalize from a particular. On the other hand, it might be valid to assume from this story that speaking in tongues is a necessary evidence of the infilling of the Holy Spirit—but this would be strictly in the category of human assumption, not clear scriptural fact.

(17) ACTS 19:6

"And when Paul had laid his hands upon them, the Holy Ghost came on them; and they spake with tongues, and prophesied."

Once again in this account, speaking in tongues is apparently an evidence that the twelve men (or more) at Ephesus had received the Holy Spirit. The gift of tongues does not stand alone in this case, however. The men also prophesied. If we were to conclude from this passage that tongues was a necessary evidence of the infilling of the Spirit, we would have to include prophesying as well because they are named on an absolutely equal basis.

(18) EPHESIANS 5:18-21

"And be not drunk with wine, wherein is excess;
but be filled with the Spirit; Speaking to yourselves in
psalms and hymns and spiritual songs, singing and
making melody in your heart to the Lord; Giving
thanks always for all things unto God and the Father
in the name of our Lord Jesus Christ; Submitting
yourselves one to another in the fear of God."

The Apostle Paul does not simply urge us to be filled
with the Spirit. He puts it in the form of a command,
and quickly adds four results—singing to one another,
having a melody in our hearts, giving thanks to
God, and submitting to one another. No mention is
made of speaking in tongues.

CONCLUSION

These are the eighteen major passages in the Word of
God that speak about the baptism, or reception, or
filling of the Holy Spirit. Three of them connect
speaking in tongues with this experience. Fifteen of
them do not even mention tongues.

It is quite possible some will conclude that in each
of these incidents tongues is understood though
not mentioned, and therefore is necessary. Others will
study these stories and conclude that three out of
eighteen is not sufficient to be the basis of a general
rule, and therefore tongues is not necessary. Both
of these positions rest upon human assumption—the
Scriptures do not state either as a fact.

My own personal assumption, after a great deal of
prayer and study, is that speaking in tongues is
not absolutely necessary to prove that a person is
under the control of the Holy Spirit. The blessed Holy
Spirit may give this gift if he chooses. Sometimes

he does and sometimes he does not. I have never spoken in tongues and I have never sought to do so. Others have this gift; I don't.

I cannot find fault with those who choose the other assumption—that speaking in tongues is a necessary evidence. The vitally important scriptural fact is that all of us who are believers need to let the Third Person of the Trinity fill and control our lives.

PART THREE
The Solution of the Church: Love

CHAPTER TEN
FROM TONGUES
TO LOVE

The topic of glossalalia (speaking in tongues) may be one of the most explosive in our times and one that leads to perhaps a greater variety of interpretations than any other subject. In contrast, no one has ever questioned the biblical fact that the fruit of love is of far greater importance than any of the spiritual gifts, including the ability to speak in tongues.

That is why I have deliberately skipped over the thirteenth chapter of First Corinthians and dealt with chapter 14 before reverting once again to the chapter that may be the Apostle Paul's best-known piece of literature—as he was guided and directed, of course, by the Holy Spirit.

Paul's own introduction to this Love chapter is to say, "and yet show I unto you a more excellent way" (1 Corinthians 12:31). Perhaps we should permit one another to have varying interpretations about the use of the gift of tongues or any other of the dramatic gifts—that is, as long as the interpretation can be supported by the teaching of the Bible on the subject. In the preceding chapters, I have attempted to outline the rather clear description that the Apostle Paul has given both about the nature of the gift of tongues and its divinely appointed use in any Christian assembly. A very stern stand should be taken against the misuse of any of the gifts of the Spirit and if our services are not conducted in a manner that can be backed up by Scripture, then, of course, we are transgressing the commandment of the Holy Spirit.

Paul's chapter on love is so dynamic that it seems to say that if this area of our lives is scripturally and practically correct, other areas will fall naturally into their proper place. However, it also teaches that if our lives do not line up to some extent satisfactorily with the teaching here, then any or all of the gifts that we might believe we possess and attempt to demonstrate are of absolutely no value.

There are many ways in which this chapter can be outlined. However, I see it as being presented in three sections. The first talks about the power of love in relation to other types of power. The second goes into a rather detailed description of the way in which love should be demonstrated in our everyday lives. The final section assesses the lasting value of several spiritual gifts and fruits as they relate to one another. For the sake of easy recall, I have used the three words dynamic, definition, and durability to describe these three sections of this chapter, and I propose to take three separate chapters and attempt to deal in an expository fashion with each of these.

But first I want to lay a doctrinal basis for the thirteenth chapter of First Corinthians by studying the source of love as explained in the fifth chapter of Romans. This will also give us a fourfold alliteration, which usually pleases a homiletical mind—derivation, dynamic, definition, and duration.

CHAPTER ELEVEN
THE DERIVATION
OF LOVE

Philosophers, authors, and psychologists have attempted to define love—its symptoms, its emotions, its effects. Generally they have failed because they have started and finished on the human level. The only authoritative definition of love is found in the Bible. That definition is accurate because it starts with God, and then describes the effects.

Many passages in the Bible deal with love. As a matter of fact, it is one of the dominant topics from Genesis through Revelation. The most pointed chapter is the thirteenth of First Corinthians. Here the Apostle Paul gives us a close-up on love. It is as if he pressed the button of a zoom lens and brought love into sharp focus on a very large screen.

Before we attempt to analyze the very practical description that we find in the Love Chapter, it is of paramount importance that we lay an adequate foundation without which the beautiful thoughts of this Pauline epistle are meaningless. Perhaps the best way to do this would be to move back into the theological and doctrinal epistle that the Apostle Paul wrote to the church at Rome, where he expresses it this way:

"Therefore being justified by faith, we have peace with God through our Lord Jesus Christ: By whom also we have access by faith into this grace wherein we stand, and rejoice in hope of the glory of God. And not only so, but we glory in tribulations also: Knowing that tribulation worketh patience; And patience, experience; and experience, hope: And hope maketh not ashamed; because the love of God is shed abroad in our hearts by the Holy Ghost which is given unto us" (Romans 5:1-5).

To make this passage more simple, I would suggest that we condense it by putting together the first verse and the last half of the fifth verse: "Therefore being justified by faith, we have peace with God through our Lord Jesus Christ . . . the love of God is shed abroad in our hearts by the Holy Ghost which is given unto us."

The first of these verses describes our position in Christ, and this is where Christian faith always begins. An individual has personal contact with the living God only through faith in Jesus Christ. Without this relationship there is no such thing as Christianity. We're not talking about our relationship with other people, but about the justification of a sinful person before God. If we do not have this kind of contact with God, all the other suggestions and beautiful precepts of the New Testament are an absolute impossibility.

The last part of verse 5 has to do with our relationship to other people in the world. It is the love of God "shed abroad in our hearts by the Holy Ghost" which makes it possible for us to relate properly to other people at home, on the street, in school, at work, etc.

The unfortunate thing about a great theological passage such as this is that most people leave it exactly where they found it—in the pages of the Bible. Sometimes we hear magnificent sermons based on this passage—sermons which bless our hearts and inspire us and make us glad we went to church. But in many cases we leave the sermons where we heard them—in the church.

All of us need to remember that outside the walls
of our sanctuaries and beyond the covers of our Bibles
there is a world of men and women, many of
whom are still waiting to see a Christian who actually
demonstrates the love of God in his everyday life.
Some of these people live in our homes; others live on
the streets where we live; they go to school with
us and often do business with us every day. But they
have been disillusioned about Christianity in general
because they have heard a great deal of theology
but seen very little of its practical effects. Sometimes
we have talked a good church and lived a bad life.
Our doctrine has been orthodox, but our actions
have sometimes been despicable.

I am sure that the Apostle Paul understood that this
would likely happen, and perhaps it was for this
reason that when he wrote to the Corinthians, he took
the time to describe in rather minute detail the
practical value, application, and durability of the love
of God. This love should be seen from day to day in
the life of any individual who has in fact been justified
by faith and has peace with God.

There are two kinds of people who read the Bible. I
sometimes refer to them as "Romans believers"
and "Corinthians believers."

The first group consists of people who are
doctrinally sound, devoted to their Bibles, and loyal
to their churches. Generally they are involved in
the activities of the church. They may be choir
members, Sunday school teachers, superintendents,
elders, deacons, etc. However, the people who live
with them and do business with them feel that all of
their Christianity is confined within the walls
of the church sanctuary and very little, if any, is

demonstrated on the streets where they live.

This kind of person appears to be an excellent Sunday school teacher, but she is an extremely cantankerous woman. He poses as a pillar of the church, but he is a pest to his business associates. They sing somewhat like angels, but act rather like the devil.

The "Romans believers" have learned a great deal about the power of God, but they have never learned how to hitch that power to the wheels of their everyday lives.

The "Corinthians believers" have been overwhelmed by the beauty and majesty of the thirteenth chapter of Paul's first letter to the Corinthian church. Their immediate reaction is, "This is the kind of person I would like to be." Then they set out to do it under their own steam. They are determined to go out into the world and love everybody and everything.

This is the one side of the Christian message that some of our modern young people have learned well. As a result, they make a great deal of use of the word love. They may paint it on the side of a panel truck, or write it on the walls of buildings, or wear it on a button on their lapel. They may even sit together in a city park just to think about it—a "love-in."

Unfortunately, it is impossible for a human being to love everybody because not everybody is lovable. It is a fact of life that there are a great many nasty people in the world—people who are mean and virtually impossible to love. That is why people who have read only the thirteenth chapter of First Corinthians soon discover that the concepts of this masterpiece of divine inspiration are not only fantastic but fantastically impossible, and it is not very long before they discover that they do not have the

kind of power that enables them to love everybody
—not in themselves.

The only way the Love Chapter of the Bible can
become a reality in any of our lives is for us to go
back to the fifth chapter of Romans and make sure
that we are in contact with God and, therefore, with
the source of power that can shed his love abroad
in our hearts, making it possible for us to accomplish
the impossible.

Complete Christians are a combination of Romans
and Corinthians. They are in contact with the living
God through faith in Jesus Christ, and their lives
demonstrate the fact that the love of God is an
active force in their hearts because of the Holy Ghost.
In one of my Bibles I have a note in the margin
beside the fifth chapter of Romans: "See 1 Corinthians
13." Then I have a note beside 1 Corinthians 13:
"See Romans 5." Each chapter is a commentary on
the other.

The love of God does not come naturally from our
human natures, which actually lead us often in the
opposite direction. Love comes out of our personal
relationship with God, resulting in justification, peace
with God, and the love of God being "shed abroad in
our hearts by the Holy Ghost which is given unto us."

CHAPTER TWELVE
THE DYNAMIC
OF LOVE

The great apostle draws attention to the dynamic of love by talking about four outstanding things that are less powerful than love—ministry, miracles, money, and martyrdom.

MINISTRY

Love is more dynamic than ministry. The word "ministry" may be a very broad term, but I am using it in the more narrow sense of the ability to communicate the message of God through our voices. "Though I speak with the tongues of men and of angels, and have not love.. I am nothing" (verses 1, 2).

All of us are familiar with the fantastic power of the human voice. During the days of the Second World War, at least three world statesmen depended very much on their ability to speak either to individuals or large crowds of people and influence them. Adolf Hitler was the megalomaniacal dictator of Germany and most of Europe, but there is no way that one can read any of his biographies without realizing the unbelievable oratorical power he had. Sometimes he used it to change the minds of his military generals. Often it was the magic instrument that stimulated the activities of millions of people.

In the United States at the same time, Franklin Roosevelt became famous for his "fireside chats." This was an entirely different kind of talking, but it was the use of the tongue of a man to influence the thoughts and the actions of a nation.

At the very same time, Sir Winston Churchill used his voice in still another manner to bolster the courage of the British people during the years that they were resisting their European enemy virtually by themselves. A great many illustrations could be given, but here are three men in one short period of history who made a never to be forgotten impact with the use of their tongues.

Paul is affirming that love is more powerful or more dynamic than even the greatest human voice.

If human speech is a potent force, it is reasonable to conclude that an angelic tongue might be even more powerful. But even the tongue of an angel falls far short of the effectiveness of love. As a matter of fact, without the motivation of love both the tongues of men and of angels give a discordant sound that jars the nerves and accomplishes very little of permanent value.

This principle may be seen rather dramatically when we visit a friend who has suffered bereavement. Usually we attempt to say something that is suitable, but we find it most difficult to adequately express ourselves. If we do manage to say something that might be important, it is often completely lost to the persons whose hearts are broken and they likely will not remember a word of it. However, they will remember that somebody loved them enough to bother coming. Love is more dynamic than ministry.

Paul is not thinking only of the power of the human tongue, but more particularly of the power of the human tongue to proclaim great and accurate spiritual truths. He connects this speaking with "the gift of prophecy"—that is, the ability to proclaim the message of God. However, even with this fantastic gift he makes it clear that it is of no value to the one who possesses it and uses it unless he or she is motivated by love. This does not mean that the proclamation of the truth will be of no value to those who hear it and receive it. Paul is simply stating that the exercise of this gift without the motivating power of love is of no value whatsoever to the speaker himself.

This principle perhaps explains the "Elmer Gantry" kind of preacher who is totally insincere himself but manages to help a great many other people. Sometimes God will bless the proclamation of his Word regardless of the character or life of the speaker.

Furthermore, the ministry about which Paul is speaking here involves a man who understands "all mysteries." That is, he has a firm grasp of the teachings of the Word of God regarding matters that for many centuries have been hidden but are now revealed.

Finally, in this context Paul indicates that the ministry involved is by one who has "all knowledge" —that is, a very firm and complete comprehension of the teachings of the Scriptures. But, despite all of these things—the tongues of men and angels, the gift of prophecy, an understanding of mysteries, and a great deal of knowledge—the exercise of these gifts is of no value whatsoever to the speaker: as a matter of fact, Paul says if he were to have these without love, he would have to say "I am nothing." Love is more dynamic than ministry.

MIRACLES

Love is more dynamic than the ability to perform

miracles—"and though I have all faith, so that I could remove mountains . . ." (verse 2). The context of these words makes it clear that the apostle is not talking about saving faith but rather miracle-working faith—the kind of faith that Jesus was talking about when he said, "If ye have faith as a grain of mustard seed, ye shall say unto this mountain, Remove hence to yonder place; and it shall remove; and nothing shall be impossible unto you" (Matthew 17:20).

It is possible to be a remarkable person in the eyes of many people, even to the extent of actually being able to perform miracles, and at the same time be absolutely nothing in the eyes of God. The test of a man's spirituality is not his ability to perform miracles of any kind. The miracle worker who is not personally right with God and filled with the love of God may certainly be helpful to thousands of people but as far as he is concerned, he must say with the Apostle Paul, "I am nothing."

MONEY

Love is more dynamic than money. "And though I bestow all my goods to feed the poor . . . and have not charity, it profiteth me nothing" (verse 3).

In his second epistle to the church at Corinth, the Apostle Paul lists giving among the graces of the Christian life, along with faith, love, etc. But here he makes it very clear that giving is of no value whatsoever to the giver unless it is motivated by the love of God.

Unfortunately, some of our giving has nothing whatever to do with love. Very often the business executive writes out a check for the United Fund in order to get rid of another business executive who is pestering him. In this case the giver has little thought about the needs of the people upon whom the money will be spent. He is not giving because he loves anybody or anything. He is giving to "get someone off his back." Of course his money will in fact help the people upon whom it is spent, but he himself will gain nothing.

In other cases, our giving is motivated purely by the incentive of a tax deduction. That is why many churches have a much higher income during the latter weeks of December than they do during other months. Certainly it is valid for a Christian to take advantage of whatever income tax deduction may be possible as a result of his giving; but if this is the only motivating force, then although the gift may prove to be a great blessing in the ministry of the church, it will be of no spiritual value to the giver.

Some of us give in order to "save face." When the offering basket is passed, it may be somewhat embarrassing if our friends notice that we put nothing in it. Therefore, we at least make the gesture with a dime, a quarter, or a dollar bill. Once again, this money will be a blessing in the ministry of the church, but it will be no blessing to the giver because it was not motivated by the love of God. "It profiteth me nothing."

MARTYRDOM

Love is more dynamic than martyrdom. "And though I give my body to be burned, and have not charity, it profiteth me nothing" (verse 3).

It is extremely dangerous to conclude that because a man gives his life for a great cause or for his country, he automatically insures himself of God's blessing. Unless his act is motivated by the love of God, his death may result in benefit to some good cause, but it is of no value to the martyr. "It profiteth me nothing."

CONCLUSION

These verses do not in any way condemn these things. The Apostle Paul would probably be the first to recognize the tremendous value of ministry, of miracles, of money, and of martyrdom—but if these are to be of any value to the person who is involved, they must be motivated by the love of God.

This is only possible through a commitment of our lives to Jesus Christ. It is then that we can say: "I am justified by faith. I have peace with God through the Lord Jesus Christ. The love of God is shed abroad in my heart by the Holy Ghost." In other words, before the actions of the outer man begin to count, the inner man must be changed.

CHAPTER THIRTEEN
THE DEFINITION
OF LOVE

Paul's definition of how the love of God operates in
the everyday life of a justified person commences
in the context of suffering: "Charity suffereth long,
and is kind."

(I'm sure you realize that the King James word
"charity" in 1 Corinthians 13 is the old English
equivalent of our modern-day word "love."
Consequently, from this point I will use "love" in
quoting from that chapter.)

LOVE SUFFERS

The love of God shed abroad in our hearts by the
Holy Ghost should give us a capacity to suffer.
Of course, no one lives very long in this world before
he discovers that life on earth inevitably involves
tribulation and hardship. Everybody knows pain at
some time in some way.

A number of years ago I preached a sermon on
suffering in my own church in Toronto. It was Sunday
morning, and the service was broadcast over one
of our local radio stations. On the following Tuesday
I received a letter from a lady who said she had heard
the broadcast, and—well, I just did not know what
I was talking about. She amplified what she meant by
giving me a description of her background.

She had been reared in a very poor home. Often at
mealtime as a child she would approach the table
to find that there was nothing on it, and no hope of

food for the next meal. She had suffered the pangs of an empty stomach. Her clothes had been extremely shabby, and she was so ashamed of them that she deliberately chose to go to school on the side streets so only a few people would see her. She had suffered the embarrassment of poor clothing. She described several occasions on which a knock at the front door had resulted in her entire family being forced out of their house and into the streets because they had not been able to pay their rent. She had suffered the blast of exposure.

After she had described these things, she pointed out that I had never been hungry, I had always had proper clothing to wear, and at no time in my life had I been without a roof over my head. All of these things were quite true. Her conclusion was that she had suffered and I had not.

This dear lady had made the same mistake that all of us have a tendency to make—that is, to conclude that the only kind of suffering is our kind and if other people have not suffered as we have suffered, they have not suffered at all. However, we need to remember that everybody experiences hurt of one kind or another. It is true that some people suffer from an empty stomach—and that is unfortunate. I would not minimize it. However, there are other people who suffer from an empty life. Who is to say which is worse?

There are those who know the pain of an aching back. Every step that they take is sheer agony, and for years they have not been able to straighten up. This too is bad. There are others who have a back as straight as a ramrod, but have an aching heart. Which is worse—the aching back or the aching heart? There are some men who have suffered because they have never been able to find a wife to marry. And this may be bad, but there are other men who have suffered because they *did* find a wife to marry.

Some people suffer because they have never been able to afford to buy a home in which to live, while others face the hardship of not knowing how to live in the home they have bought.

It is unlikely that any two people ever suffer in exactly the same manner, but one of the facts of life is that we do suffer; and Paul is reminding the Christians at Corinth that if they really have been justified by faith and if the love of God is in fact shed abroad in their hearts by the Holy Ghost, then they should have a godly capacity for suffering.

Love Suffers Long. In the Greek there is just one word used here which expresses the idea of suffering a long time. That is why most of the more modern translations simply use the single English word "patient." However, whether we read from the King James Version, one of the other translations, or the original Greek, the meaning is precisely the same: The love of God shed abroad in the heart of a person by the Holy Ghost gives that person the capacity not only to suffer, but to endure suffering if necessary over a long period of time. In the construction of this sentence in any language, there is no period or full stop at the end of the word or words used. This should perhaps remind us that the duration of our suffering is not to be determined by us, but rather it is in the hands of God. It is our impatience that leads us to believe there is a time at which we have a right to say, "I have had enough."

The Elder and His Son. Some years ago one of my

elders came into my office, obviously in a very agitated
condition. After he had calmed down to some extent,
I asked him what was the matter. I shall never
forget the way he lifted a large working man's fist,
dropped it with a thud on my desk, and said, "Pastor,
I've done it!" He then proceeded to tell me what
he had done.

Apparently he had been having some difficulties
with his seventeen-year-old son for quite some time.
The boy would go out at night and although he was
aware of a required curfew, he never came home on
time. Each night it was becoming later and later.
The day before this elder came to see me, he had had a
conference with his son in which he had given him
an ultimatum: he was to come in that night at a
certain hour and if he did not arrive on time, the front
door would be locked and the son would have to
find another place to live.

That night this is precisely what happened. The
father gave the son a little extra time, but finally in
complete exasperation he got up and went to the
front door and locked it. As he sat before me, he
declared that his son was gone and he did not know
where. The sequel to this story is that that particular
son never did return to his home, and by shutting
him out his father had lost whatever opportunity he
might have had of communicating with him in any
way in the years that have passed since that time.

The problem with this elder's theology is common
to all of us. He knew that he could expect some
difficulties from a teenaged boy. He understood that
a forty-five-year-old man would not always see eye to
eye with a seventeen-year-old son. He was quite
ready to accept a certain amount of suffering from this
direction. However, he had the idea in the back of

his mind that somewhere along the line he had the right to say, "I have had enough. I have taken as much as I can take. This suffering has got to end."

He had completely forgotten that the love of God shed abroad in the heart of a justified person not only suffers but goes on suffering, and God determines how long it will last. It may be for a day or for a week or for a month or, in some cases, it could be for a lifetime.

Every intelligent Christian is aware of the fact that what Paul has said so far does not in any particular way describe only a Christian. All of us know that many people who are not Christians at all suffer a great deal, and some of them suffer a very long time. There are members of most of the other religions in the world who may know practically nothing about the love of God who have sustained severe suffering for a lifetime. That is why Paul adds this next thought.

LOVE IS KIND

It is important at this point to remember that the kindness is not standing by itself. Rather, it is connected with hardship. Long-suffering is a negative attitude toward difficulty, whereas kindness is a positive attitude toward exactly the same thing. The Christian not only sustains suffering in a sort of negative manner, but he has the God-given capacity to turn about and actually be kind to the source of his suffering. The same concept is expressed in many different places in the New Testament, for example: "Therefore if thine enemy hunger, feed him; if he thirst, give him drink: for in so doing thou shalt heap coals of fire on his head" (Romans 12:20).

The "coals of fire" are symbolic of the judgment of

God. When a good man is kind to a bad man, it makes the contrast between the two much more apparent. Thus, the unrighteous person becomes more conscious of his own guilt and his impending doom, and this deep conviction may lead him to get right with God. The best way to win people to Christ is to return good for evil, blessing for cursing, healing for wounding. We may bring about conviction by condemning a man's sin, but we are more likely to do so by living such a holy life that it stands in stark contrast to his life of evil.

Our natural reaction to injury is to retaliate. Jesus taught us that love and retaliation are opposites.

In countries that had been conquered by the Roman Empire, a soldier could compel anybody to carry a load for a maximum of one mile. This was the law and, of course, Jews hated it and rebelled against it. Jesus told them that the next time they were asked to go one mile by a Roman soldier, they should not only do it gladly, but offer to go a second mile (Matthew 5:41). If the Jew in question had been one of the early Christians, can you imagine how easy it would have been for him to have explained the claims of Jesus Christ to that Roman soldier at the end of the second mile. Effective witnessing begins at the end of the second mile. That's what the love of God is all about. It produces a kind of person whose way of living opens locked doors and allows him to enter with the gospel.

This sort of reaction to difficulty separates Christians from non-Christians. People who know nothing of the love of God go the first mile reluctantly, belligerently, with hatred controlling their hearts. Christians go the first mile willingly, peacefully, with love in their hearts. Then they look for an opportunity to carry the load still farther—and a chance to talk to someone about Jesus Christ. World missions begins at the end of the second mile.

This is the disarming power of love that leaves its enemies without defense and may lead them to seek the Savior. Love bears affliction for a long time and is kind to those who cause it.

LOVE ENVIES NOT

The dictionary defines envy as "pain at the sight of the superior excellence in another." This usually results in a malicious feeling toward the more excellent person—sometimes because of possessions, sometimes because of ability, sometimes because of accomplishments.

Envy is not quite the same as jealousy, although they are related. Jealousy is fear of losing something that we already possess. Envy involves a desire to possess something that really belongs to another and to which we have no right. For instance, if I were a teenager "going steady" with a teenaged girl and she were beginning to show an interest in you, the feeling that I would have toward you would be one of jealousy—the fear of losing my sweetheart.

On the other hand, if the girl was "going steady" with you and I felt that I wanted her, the feeling that I would have toward you would be envy.

The English word "envy" comes from the Latin *invidere*—"to look askance at, to see." A good example of this feeling and the use of this word is found in the story of King Saul and David. Saul had always been a great warrior and was very much admired by his subjects. However, David proved to be an even greater warrior. After battles in which both of these men were involved, the people would line the path as they returned. When they saw King Saul approaching, they would cry out, "Saul hath slain his thousands." Of course, this was very pleasing to the ears of the King. But just as he was beginning to revel in it, David would appear and the people would cry out in louder voices, "and David his ten thousands."

Then the Bible says, "And Saul eyed David from that day and forward" (1 Samuel 18:9). In the ancient Latin translation, the Septuagint, the word used for "eyed" was *invidia*.

This simply meant that King Saul turned around and looked at David maliciously with an intent to do him harm when the occasion arose. This is envy, with a feeling of animosity toward another because of superior qualifications of one kind or another.

When translators are working from a Hebrew manuscript, the English word "envy" is often a translation of some form of the Hebrew word *qinah*. The original meaning is "burning," and the connection between this word and our modern English word "envy" can be seen to some extent in some of our figures of speech. For instance, we often use the expression, "That burns me up." Or we might refer to a person as being "hot under the collar." In these instances we are attempting to describe the feelings of a person toward the actions, possessions, or abilities of someone else.

It is important at this point that we should be aware of those things which should not be construed as envy. If a man sees his neighbor's new Cadillac and wishes he had one too, he is not being envious but quite normal. If the same man resents his neighbor's good fortune and is malicious toward him because of it, he is envious.

If I hear a great preacher and say to myself, "I wish I could preach like that," that is not envy. But if the accomplishment of a great preacher irritates me and makes me dislike him, that is envy.

If a girl sees her best friend come to a party wearing a mink stole and she thinks, "I'd like to have one of those," that is not envy. If her friend's mink stole spoils the party for her, that is envy.

The Christian should never get "burned up" over the accomplishments or the possessions of others. If we do, to that extent we are failing to demonstrate the love of God and are perhaps losing an opportunity to point someone to Christ.

LOVE DOESN'T SHOW OFF

"Showing off" and acting like a Christian are the antitheses of one another. The "show-off" is thinking only of himself; the Christian is concerned about serving God and helping others.

"Love vaunteth not itself" (verse 4). The *Phillips* translation says love is not "anxious to impress." *The New English Bible* suggests, "Love is never boastful." *The Amplified Bible* tells us that love "does not display itself haughtily."

Jesus commented on the same human trait when he said, "Take heed that ye do not your alms before men, to be seen of them" (Matthew 6:1).

This does not mean that a Christian should not have confidence in the ability God has given. If a Christian girl has a beautiful voice, she should not try to convince people that she is really just an average singer. This would be false modesty and would border on lying. She should use her gift with confidence, though strictly for the glory of God. If she sings to impress the public, she is showing off. "Love vaunteth not itself."

LOVE IS NOT EGOTISTICAL

The same verse that says, "Love vaunteth not itself" adds that love "is not puffed up."

These two are not quite the same. The first has to do with a demonstration on the outside. The second has to do with a feeling on the inside. The first can be seen by others. The second cannot be seen.

It is something like a balloon. The colored rubber which looks so glamorous is the "vaunting." The air on the inside is the "puffing up." The point of a pin proves in an instant that the whole thing was mere display; there was no real substance. It was just rubber stretched around a bit of air.

Love in the hearts of Christians prevents them from being egotistical. They are not inflated with a sense of their own importance. They serve God gladly, using with confidence the gifts that he has given them—but they do so with a sense of humility and complete dependence upon God. Love "is not puffed up."

At this point most of us have a tendency to think of people to whom these things apply. All of us can think of friends who have a tendency to be envious. We can think of all kinds of people who in our opinion are show-offs, and we are quite ready to classify a great many other people as egotistical. However, we need to remember that this passage applies to each one of us. This chapter was written to Christian people, and under certain conditions all of us have a tendency to be envious, to show off, and to be egotistical. There are very few people who are guilty of these things all the time, but all of us are guilty of

them some of the time. These are the human
potentials of all Christians.

LOVE HAS GOOD MANNERS

The King James Version says love "doth not behave
itself unseemly" (verse 5). *Phillips* translates it,
"Love has good manners." *The Living Bible* pictures
love as "never haughty or selfish or rude." *The New
American Standard Bible* tells us love "does not act
unbecomingly." Both *The New English Bible* and *The
Revised Standard Version* express this idea with
the word "rude."

Obviously the Apostle Paul is talking about our
manners in every area of life. When a man commits his
life to Jesus Christ, he is not only justified, but
he also becomes a gentleman. When a woman accepts
Christ, she is not only born into the family of God, but
she becomes a lady. Wherever they go and whatever
they are called upon to do, Christians are people who
have good manners.

This does not mean that the young convert must
buy the latest book on etiquette. However, in some
cases such a procedure might not do any harm. If
any book on etiquette is analyzed, it will be discovered
that there is one common denominator to manners
in any country and at any time in history—namely,
acting in such a way that we do not unnecessarily
offend the sensitivities of other people.

In the Orient, table manners involve the use of
chopsticks. In India and many parts of Africa, they
involve the use of certain fingers. In Europe and
North America, we generally use knives and forks,
although Europeans have an entirely different way of
using them than do most North Americans. Basically,

these implements are not designed primarily to facilitate the transport of food from one's plate to one's mouth. As a matter of fact, they make it much more difficult. If you do not believe this, ask any panel of babies and they will tell you that it is much easier simply to use the hands that God has given without having to go through the arduous process of learning how to use chopsticks or fingers or cutlery in a prescribed manner.

Although it might be a great deal easier to use our hands and dispense with the cutlery, it would not be very long before we would have an extremely limited number of friends with whom to eat. We would have offended their sensitivities by our sloppy and uncouth manner of eating.

We offend the sensitivities of other people if we travel in a foreign country and completely disregard the local manners and customs and culture. This is pointed out sharply by William J. Lederer and Eugene Burdick in *The Ugly American*. This is a fictitious story of some members of the U. S. diplomatic corps who had very little thought for the way of life in the country where they served, and as a result did irreparable damage to the image and prestige of the United States. This should be required reading for every missionary who crosses cultures.

Of course, this kind of book could have been written about some diplomats from all countries. It could easily have been *The Ugly Russian*, *The Ugly Canadian*, *The Ugly Englishman*, etc. Perhaps one should be written on *The Ugly Tourist*. There are some people who seem to feel that every other nation should be exactly like their own, and if it is not they assume that the people are simply ignorant. These are the kind of tourists that spoil the reputation of their own country because they do not have good manners—they act in an unbecoming way—they are not sensitive to the feelings of other people.

Unfortunately, there are some Christian people who act in such a manner that it becomes impossible for them to witness effectively. If I have been rude to someone with whom I live, it is a waste of time for me to try to win that person to Jesus Christ. If I offend the sensitivities of the neighbors on my street, there is no point in asking them to go to church. If I am ill-mannered with someone with whom I work, there will be no opportunity for me to explain "The Four Spiritual Laws" to him. If I go to another country as a missionary and show disrepect for the culture of that people, I might as well pack my bags and go home. In each of these cases, the door is just not open. I have closed it myself.

I must not be insensitive to those I am trying to win. Of course, if there is a moral principle involved, then I may be compelled to hurt someone's feelings. My duty to obey God's law has priority over my obligation to avoid offending other people.

When we are justified by faith, the love of God is shed abroad in our hearts in such a way that we are able to move out into our society and be effective witnesses for Jesus Christ because we have good manners—we do not unnecessarily offend other people.

LOVE IS NOT SELFISH

The next phrase follows very naturally from the one just before it. As a matter of fact, the two are contingent upon each other. Without doing violence to the Scriptures, it could be read in this way: "Love doth not behave itself unseemly because love seeketh not her own."

The New English Bible tells us love is "never selfish." *The Revised Standard Version* says, "Love does not insist on its own way." *Phillips* puts it, "Love . . . does not pursue selfish advantage." The only people who can really be sensitive to the feelings of other people are those who forget about themselves. This way of living stands in stark contrast to our materialistically minded world. Generally we have a tendency to ask the questions, "What do I get out of it? What's in it for me? How much does it pay?" Unfortunately, even in the serious business of choosing a profession these questions are uppermost in our minds.

The Christian approach should not be, "What do I get out of it?" but rather, "How much can I put into it? How can I contribute some of my life to this very needy world, so that when it is all over, the world will be a better place in some respects because I was in it?" Christianity involves an opportunity to be of service in our homes, on our streets, in our cities, and throughout the world.

LOVE DOES NOT HAVE HURT FEELINGS

The Authorized Version renders the next phrase, "is not easily provoked." Phillips prefers, love "is not touchy." *The Revised Standard Version* translates it, love "is not irritable or resentful." *The New English Bible* says love is "not quick to take offence."

Putting these all together we might paraphrase the thought with the words, "Love does not get its feelings hurt." Once again, this follows directly from the former. If I am constantly looking out for my own welfare, there will be many times when I will be left out or forgotten or ignored, and then I will have every opportunity of becoming angry. We could tie these three thoughts together in this way: "Love does not behave itself unseemly because love seeketh not her own and therefore love is not easily provoked."

Perhaps the best antidote for hurt feelings is to become involved in something which is much more important than any individual person. If politicians and statesmen did not do this, they could not survive for a week with the barrage of criticism that is leveled against them almost every day. Most of us have a tendency to be "floored" when one or two nasty comments come our way, let alone being condemned in the headlines of the daily newspapers constantly.

The only reason that politicians are able to go on is that in most cases they are involved in some kind of a cause that they consider much more important than themselves. In some cases, it is a political party. Sometimes it is patriotic. In other situations, it is some great principle that is involved. Whatever it is, they are able to say, "I do not really care what you say about me as long as the cause for which I stand goes forward."

Can you think of anybody in the world that has a greater cause in which to be involved than the child of God? We have the gospel of Jesus Christ—the power of God which is able to come into the life of a man or a woman and change it completely. We have the answer to the needs of the world. We have the solution to sin and guilt. We have the only basis for peace of heart. In the Lord Jesus Christ, the Christian has the solution for which the people of the world are searching. Sad to say, many of us spend too much of our time feeling sorry for ourselves instead of throwing ourselves into the work and becoming lost in the cause.

In three of the Gospel records, Jesus compares his
people to salt. Can you imagine a conversation which
might go on between two grains of salt as they
nestle comfortably in their saltshaker:

"Isn't it lovely in here. Look, we are all the same
size, the same color, and the same shape. Let's just
stay here and enjoy ourselves."

"But the cook wants us in the soup."

"Do you know what it's like in that soup? There are
great, big, boiled potatoes. Have you ever tried to
swim around a boiled potato? Then there are huge
orange carrots. Can you imagine what it would be like
to be smashed by a carrot?"

"But our whole purpose in this world is to get into
that soup."

"But look how lovely it is here. Notice the beautiful
amber stained glass windows and that magnificent
silver dome that protects us from the elements. Let's
just stay here and sing another hymn and read a
few more verses of Scripture."

Certainly it is true that there is a place and a time
for the security of the saltshaker. The Christian
needs the fellowship and edification of the local
church. This is a scriptural principle. The Bible is very
clear about the fact that there is to be a local
congregation of believers who meet in a specific place
at a certain time and for a particular purpose. That
is one of the reasons that the writer of the book of
Hebrews urges us not to forsake "the assembling of
ourselves together" (10:25). That is why a major part
of the New Testament is directed toward churches or
the ministers of churches. However, along with these
great passages that authorize the establishment of the
local church are the constant injunctions of the
Word of God that Christians need to move into the

world and bear their witness for Jesus Christ.

Perhaps the greatest condemnation that can be leveled at the church over the centuries is that too often we have said the same things using the same cliches to the same people, with very little attempt to make our testimony heard outside of the stained glass windows of our ecclesiastical saltshakers.

It should be noted that when the salt enters the soup, the soup does not immediately turn to salt. However, the entire character of every drop of that soup is changed with the introduction of the first grain of salt. When you become a child of God, that does not mean that every member of your household will automatically be saved. It does mean that when you go home the character of that household will be forever changed. Your family may be the only Christians in your block. This does not mean that eventually every other household will become Christian. It does mean that the character of your street will be forever changed because your family lives there.

The Christians who remain forever in the saltshaker will probably have their feelings hurt eventually. But the Christians whose lives are edified by fellowship with other Christians in the saltshaker and then move out into the soup of the world will not have too much time to cry over themselves. If I have been justified by faith and the love of God has been shed abroad in my heart by the Holy Ghost, then I will not be subject to hurt feelings—love "is not easily provoked."

LOVE DOES NOT KEEP SCORE

The last phrase in verse five is really a thought that stands by itself—love "thinketh no evil."

The Living Bible paraphrases this, "It does not hold grudges and will hardly even notice when others do it wrong."

The New American Standard Bible translates it: "does not take into account a wrong suffered."

Phillips says, "It does not keep account of evil."

The New English Bible has it, "Love keeps no score of wrongs."

In the vernacular this simply means love does not keep score.

I do not play a very good game of golf. It is all I can do to break 120. This means that for most of my game I am anywhere but on the fairway, and usually I am lying about six or eight when I get on the green. However, sometimes I am lucky and by the eighteenth hole I manage to make a par. When I do this I cannot help but turn excitedly to the men who are playing with me and brag about the fact that I parred the eighteenth.

It is at this point that one of my friends inevitably pulls the scorecard out of his pocket and says, "Smith, you've parred the eighteenth but remember, you blew the first seventeen." And that generally spoils the entire game for me. It makes me wish that we could play golf without keeping score. Of course this is not possible. But what the Apostle Paul is pointing out in this passage is that in the game of life, the person who is justified by faith and in whose heart the love of God has been shed abroad does not need to keep score.

Marriage relationships, business alliances, and sometimes long friendships have come to a disastrous end because one of the people involved insisted upon keeping score on the other. When a marriage breaks up after many years, usually the cause that is given is not sufficient to warrant it, and we sometimes wonder why it happened. In reality, the marriage was not dissolved because of that one thing in particular. It just happened to be the final entry on a very long scorecard. It was the proverbial "straw that broke the camel's back."

No human relationship can stand the pressure of a scorecard. What chance would a mother have if her children insisted upon keeping score over the years and registering everything about her that they did not like? What chance of survival would children have if their parents kept a careful record of all their little misdemeanors? They simply could not survive.

The Apostle Paul is making an appeal to God's people—to have the courage to tear up their scorecards and put an end to the miserable habit of keeping statistics of the evil that has been done to them—love "thinketh no evil."

LOVE AND THE NEW MORALITY

In dealing with the problem of guilt we have two options: through the power of the Holy Spirit we can change our way of living so that it meets the standards of the Bible; or else we can "change" the standards of the Bible so that they correspond with our way of living.

We will either deal directly with the problem of our sin, or else we will rationalize to such an extent that eventually our sin looks like righteousness to us.

In the language of this chapter, we have a choice of rejoicing in iniquity or rejoicing in the truth. It is absolutely impossible to rejoice in sin unless we have managed to rationalize it to such an extent that we begin to call it by some other name. This procedure is

really at the base of what we call "the new morality."
It is my personal opinion that man knows intuitively
that certain things are wrong. However, even if this
were not so, the Bible states explicitly that certain
things are evil. In other words, there is a standard
which God expects us to respect.

The new morality does not accept any objective
standard of right and wrong. Activities are judged on
the basis of the situation. In some cases it might
be wrong to tell a lie, whereas in another situation it
might be quite permissible to lie. The same thing may
be said of adultery, murder, stealing, etc. This is
known as "situational ethics," and is acceptable only
to a person whose mind has been warped and twisted
by sin. This kind of mind can look at things that are
wrong and say that they are right, and can turn its
back upon things that are right and say that they are
wrong. It can actually rejoice in iniquity and fail to
rejoice in the truth.

The Apostle Paul expresses the same idea in
Philippians 3:19 where he describes godless people as
those "whose glory is in their shame." Sin has so
perverted and warped the minds of some people that
they actually boast of the things of which they should
be thoroughly ashamed. They rejoice over those things
about which they should weep. But the person who
has been justified by faith is ever conscious of what
sin did—it caused Christ to die on the cross. Of what it
is doing—it is creating the corruption present in
the world today, ruining homes and blighting lives. Of
what it will do—it leads to destruction. This, of
course, makes the justified person hate sin, and even
the thought of sin almost crushes the Christian.

This is a good test of Christianity: what makes us
rejoice? what makes us weep? The Christian rejoices

in righteousness. The person who is not a Christian revels in iniquity. The Christian loves God and his truth. The person who is not a Christian despises God and his truth. When we commit our lives to Jesus Christ, one of the immediate results is that some of the things we used to love we now hate and some of the things we used to hate we now love.

THE GREATEST VERSE

In my opinion the seventh verse of the thirteenth chapter of Paul's first letter to the Corinthians is the greatest single verse in the Bible as far as Christian people are concerned. Those tremendous passages which explain the way of salvation are certainly the most important as far as the world is concerned. However, when it comes to the child of God—the justified person—this verse has no equal. It says four things about those in whose hearts the love of God has been shed abroad: they bear all things, they believe all things, they hope all things, and they endure all things.

We should consider each of these four things from two different standpoints: (1) What do they say to me personally apart from anybody else in the world? (2) What do they say to me in regard to my relationship with other people?

Perhaps one of the most difficult tasks psychiatrists face is to teach their patients how to live with themselves. It is a fact that most of our problems do not come from other people, but from ourselves. One of the reasons that we have difficulty in getting along with the people around us is that we have never learned how to deal with ourselves.

This is natural because there are many things about

ourselves that we do not like. Sometimes we do not like our height or our weight or our financial standing or our social status or our race or our color or the shape of our faces. Most of these things we cannot change very much and if we do not learn to accept them, we will have great difficulty in living with anybody else. However, once we have learned to live with ourselves, we must face the problem of living with other people. So we must look at these from both standpoints. How do they affect me and how do they affect others?

LOVE BEARS ALL

Love "beareth all things" (verse 7). That word "beareth" is a translation of the Greek verb "*stego*," which means to cover closely. It would involve the kind of covering that would prevent any leakage. As a noun, it would often be translated by the English word "roof." The purpose of a roof is to prevent rain from leaking in, and one of the purposes of love is to prevent burdens from leaking out.

In this passage the Apostle Paul was talking about our problems. He began his definition of love in verse four with the concept of suffering, and it is in this context that he says love "beareth all things." Those who know God have the capacity to cover their burdens closely, or to put the kind of roof over them that will not allow them to leak out and affect (or even hurt) other people. A water pot "bears" water in the sense that it has the capacity to contain it without letting it fall on the ground.

There are few Christians who have this capacity. Most of us have a tendency to spill our troubles on other people, generally upon our best friends and

those we love the most. We have a great urge to
go about crying on the shoulders of other people
instead of depending on the power of God to enable us
to bear our own burdens.

It should be quickly stated that the Apostle Paul
is not talking about some of the very serious problems
of life. There are times when we face a medical
problem that is too big for us. There is no sense in
which we should attempt to contain this. We should
go to our doctor and talk about it. Sometimes we face
a serious spiritual problem that is too much for us.
With this kind of thing, we should go to our minister
and discuss it. Even Christian people may be
confronted with a grave emotional problem. The
Apostle Paul is not suggesting that we should attempt
to carry this sort of thing by ourselves. There are
professional people who are trained to help us with
this kind of difficulty.

However, the apostle is talking about the everyday
problems of life—the burdens and pains and aches
and discomforts to which we are all subject. The love
of God shed abroad in our hearts should give us
the capacity to contain these without letting them
leak out or spill over.

Then as we turn our attention from ourselves to
other people, this means that we should have the
capacity to contain *their* problems without letting
them leak out. Sad to say, even within the walls
of the Christian church it is difficult to find those
who can be trusted with other peoples' problems.
In many cases, we no sooner hear them than we are
eager to tell someone else. If someone notices that I
have the ability to bear my own burdens, then
they will see in me a confidant with whom they can
trust even the heaviest of their burdens.

In his letter to the Galatians the Apostle Paul incorporates both of these thoughts within a few verses when he says, "Bear ye one another's burdens, and so fulfil the law of Christ... For every man shall bear his own burden" (Galatians 6:2, 5).

LOVE BELIEVES

Love "believeth all things" (verse 7). The word "believeth" in this context is not concerned with the acceptance of intellectual data, but rather it has to do with looking at things with a positive attitude. In other words, love takes the best view of all things as long as it is possible to do so.

When I apply this to myself, it means that regardless of the apparent difficulties and problems I may be concerned about, I do not become preoccupied with them. Instead, I do everything within my power to focus my attention upon the blessings of my life instead of the burdens.

Someone might come to me and complain, "I'm sick." This is bad, of course, but he's not bankrupt and that is good.

Another person comes to me and says, "I'm bankrupt." This is bad, but she is not sick, and that is good.

Still another comes and says, "I am sick and bankrupt." That is doubly bad, but that person is not alone in the world. There are some people who are forced to live by themselves and when these kinds of misfortunes befall them, there is no one who really cares about them.

Another comes to me and says, "It's pouring rain outside." That may be bad, but I have an umbrella and that is good. The love of God shed abroad in our hearts should give us the capacity to count our blessings instead of our burdens. It enables us to thank God for our umbrellas rather than bemoaning the rain.

Then, as I look at the misfortunes of other people, I do for them exactly what the love of God enables me to do for myself: I take the best view as long as it is possible to do so. In the courts of much of the civilized world, we believe that regardless of the accusation a person must be considered innocent until proven guilty. However, in our everyday human relationships we have a tendency to work on the principle that other people are guilty until they have managed to prove that they are innocent—and, sad to say, we do this with the people whom we claim to love the most.

When our children go out at night, we generally give them a curfew. If they are not home by that time, we wait for a few extra minutes, and if they still do not appear, we begin making up our speech. At last when the doorbell rings and we open it, we are ready to "jump down their throats" before they have had any opportunity to explain why they are late. In other words, we have stood back with folded arms as if we were some kind of special saints and said to our children, "We think you are guilty. Go ahead and prove that you are innocent." With this kind of approach, which is far too common among parents, we have not given our children whom we claim to love the same break that they would get in a criminal court.

LOVE HOPES

Love "hopeth all things" (verse 7).

If you can bear your own infirmities and problems and those of others, if you can expect blessing for yourself and others instead of concentrating on misfortune and trials, then you have hope for a good outcome both in your life and in the lives of those around you.

When I apply this to myself, it means that regardless of the circumstances, I never reach the point where I cross myself off. I never lose hope.

I have had so many cold sores, or fever blisters, that I believe I may be the world's leading authority on them. I have discovered two basic things about cold sores. If you learn these, you will never have any more real problems from them. In the first place, I am convinced that there is no cure. I think I have tried about every remedy that has ever been suggested to me. Some of them have been so severe that they have almost burned off my lips. Some years ago when I was preaching in the state of Louisiana, a very intelligent looking businessman came up to me after a message in which I had talked about cold sores. He gave me a small tube of ointment, and then with great confidence he said, "This is the cure that you have been looking for." When I asked him how I should use it, he looked at me without even the trace of a smile and said, "All you have to do is put it on the cold sore before it appears on your lip."

The second important thing I have learned about cold sores is that if I wait about ten or twelve days, they always disappear!

Suppose when I go into the washroom tomorrow morning I notice that there is a new cold sore appearing on my lip. What do I do? Do I hang my head and cry because I know there is no cure? Not at all. I stand straight up and look that little cold sore right squarely in the eye. Then I talk to it. "Mr. Cold Sore, I know there is no cure for you. However, I am just going to wait about ten or twelve days, and in that time you are going to be gone and I am still going to be right here."

I am very much aware of the fact that among the multitudes of people who will read these pages there will be a great many cold sores—blemishes on their lives that appear to be incurable. Some people are confronted with a marital cold sore. Others are depressed by a spiritual cold sore. Still others are molested by a business cold sore. The blemish in a person's life may involve his morals, his education, his family.

May I make a suggestion to you if you suffer from one of the cold sores of life. If you are a child of God, sit straight up in your chair, look that dreadful blemish right in the eye, and talk to it. "Mr. Cold Sore, I do not know the cure. I cannot seem to find the solution. No one seems to be able to give me the answer. However, I am a Christian. I have confidence in the power of God and I am going to wait. Sometime, somewhere, somehow you are going to be gone and Almighty God and I are still going to be right here."

Is that not what the Apostle Paul was talking about in the book of Romans when he said, "And we know that all things work together for good to them that love God, to them who are the called according to his purpose" (Romans 8:28).

Love never crosses itself off, never gives up—Love "hopeth all things."

As I turn my attention to other people, I look at them with the eye of hope also. I never cross anyone else off. Have you ever noticed how often Christian people write off others? In *our* books there are hopeless people, hopeless children, hopeless parents, hopeless partners, etc., etc., etc.

As those who enjoy peace with God, we can learn

how to look at that "impossible" person with the eyes of hope. This is certainly part of the truth that Jesus was illustrating in his story of the wheat and the tares. Someone had observed that both wheat and tares were growing in the farmer's field and, of course, everyone knew that the farmer had no need of the tares. Therefore, the logical question seemed to be, "Wilt thou then that we go and gather them up?" The immediate answer was, "Nay; lest while ye gather up the tares, ye root up also the wheat with them" (Matthew 13:28, 29).

Just a few verses farther on, Jesus explained privately to his disciples that "the field is the world; the good seed are the children of the kingdom; but the tares are the children of the wicked one" (Matthew 13:38).

There may have been many reasons that the tares should not be rooted up. Two of them are quite obvious: First, it is absolutely impossible for any human being to know unerringly the difference between wheat and tares, that is, the difference between the children of God and the children of Satan. This does not mean that we cannot make a judgment about other people. It simply means that we do not know the final answer. There are really only two persons who know the spiritual condition of anyone—that person and God. Others may come close to the truth, but they can never be absolutely sure. That is why our Lord said that in the course of rooting up the tares, we might also root up some of the wheat.

In the second place, the message of the gospel reveals to us how God performs the miracle of turning tares into wheat. This is what the message of Jesus Christ is all about—the transforming power of God. In my human stupidity I may cross off some drunkard ten days before God is going to save him. I may cross off some

child ten years before God is going to call him to be a
prophet. The story of the wheat and tares tells us
that we have no right to play at being God. Love looks
at the other man through eyes of hope and never gives
up on him.

LOVE ENDURES

Love "endureth all things" (verse 7). Very little needs
to be said about this last phrase because it follows
automatically from the rest of the verse. It is hope
within the human breast that enables us to keep going.
If we do not have hope for the future at some point, we
will not be able to endure the present. When we
are robbed of our hope, eventually we will come to a
situation in the "now" of our lives that will be
intolerable and we will give up. It is because the love of
God shed abroad in our hearts enables us to look at
everything hopefully that we are able to handle the
problems and burdens of the present.

   Christians can live in the midst of a crazy world
and not go berserk themselves. Christians can be
perfectly at peace even when they are surrounded by
the sounds of battle. The world in which they live may
be completely adrift, but Christians are always
anchored. They have been justified by faith. They have
peace with God. The love of God has been shed abroad
in their hearts by the Holy Ghost and love "hopeth
all things."

CHAPTER FOURTEEN
THE DURATION
OF LOVE

The last six verses of this fantastic chapter were written
to emphasize the fact that after some of the more
dramatic gifts have passed away, love will be one of the
things that will remain. The only problem that seems to
confront students of the Bible is the question of
when this is to take place, and the most obvious answer
to this question is—at the time of the Second Coming
of our Lord. There is really no scriptural evidence to
indicate that this chapter was written to say that
love will replace tongues or any other gift during this
present period of time when the church is God's
representative in the world.

Included with tongues the apostle lists, along with
other things, prophecy, faith, humanitarianism,
and martyrdom. I doubt if anyone would suggest that a
spirit of love will eventually do away with prophesying,
faith, giving to the poor, or dying for the cause of
Christ.

The point is that if these things are not motivated
by love, they are of no value, regardless of how dramatic
they may be. This is not a denunciation of tongues
or any of these other talents, but rather a continuation
of the discussion about their place and proper use
in the work of the church. Certainly the last few verses
state emphatically that some of these things—
prophecies, tongues, knowledge, and "that which is in
part"—will come to an end; and that faith, hope,
and love will abide. The only question that might be
raised is that of time. When will these things cease?

SHORTLY AFTER THE APOSTOLIC AGE?
One school of thought suggests that in the early
church, there had to be some special revelation
through the gifts of tongues and prophesying and
miracles because the New Testament was not yet
complete. The apostles had only the Old Testament
and their own limited memory of the teaching of
Jesus. Thus Paul says, "For we know in part, and
we prophesy in part" (verse 9). Once the New
Testament was completed and in circulation, the
special gifts stopped because they were no longer
needed: "when that which is perfect is come, then
that which is in part shall be done away" (verse 10).

The two illustrations the apostle gives are tailored
to fit into this interpretation. When the church
was young (a child), it needed these dramatic
demonstrations because it only had an immature
revelation in the Old Testament. But when the church
grew up ("became a man"), by virtue of the fact
that it now had the New Testament, it "put away
childish things"—that is, it gradually outgrew the
miraculous gifts and depended solely on the completed
(perfect) Bible for its guidance.

The illustration about the mirror ("glass") is
interpreted much the same way. In the early days,
Christians had a blurred revelation because they only
had the Old Testament. Therefore, they needed the
miraculous gifts to clarify their vision. They saw
"through a glass darkly." When the New Testament
was completed, they saw clearly as if "face to face," and
the dramatic gifts were unnecessary and faded away.

In its young days, the church knew only in part
because the Bible was not yet finished. After the
apostolic period, it knew everything it needed to know
through the completed Scriptures. Therefore, there

was no further need of special revelation through tongues or prophecies or miracles.

In short, this view says that during the apostolic years the miraculous gifts were necessary because Old Testament revelation was incomplete, but with the writing of the New Testament the gifts disappeared.

AN ASSUMPTION NOT A FACT

This is an interesting interpretation and it may be quite valid. However, it should be held only as a human assumption or inference, not as scriptural fact. A careful analysis of the things about which we disagree will reveal that many of them are not based on scriptural fact at all. They have been derived from assumptions we have made on the basis of what the Word says. At this point we cannot be dogmatic, but it is unwise to wield our human inferences as if they were the sword of the Spirit.

The Bible says, "For we know in part." The interpretation given above says that this partial knowledge is the Old Testament and the oral stories of the disciples. However, this limited knowledge could just as logically refer to man's finite knowledge as opposed to God's infinite knowledge. Man simply does not know everything.

"When that which is perfect is come" is said to refer to the completion or perfection of the Bible. This is an interesting and perhaps a good assumption, but it is certainly not a necessary one. Many students of the Bible believe Paul is talking about the perfection of the church. This will not take place until it has been completed and the Lord returns. Or it could refer to the perfection of the individual Christian—a process that goes on as long as that person is in this world.

In Ephesians the apostle actually connects some of the same gifts that are under consideration in Corinthians with the process of the perfecting of the saints: "till we all come in the unity of the faith, and of the knowledge of the Son of God, unto a perfect man, unto the measure of the stature of the fulness of Christ" (4:13). Prophecy is included among the gifts that are necessary to this perfecting process.

"When I was a child" is assumed to refer to the young days of the church. "When I became a man" is taken to apply to the time spiritual things were seen because of a completed Bible. "Then face to face" is said to refer to the detailed revelation of the New Testament which made the Old Testament seem like a poorly reflected vision in a mirror.

But "now" could mean before the Lord comes, and "then" could mean after he comes. "Now" could mean in this life. "Then" could mean in the next life.

To conclude that the thirteenth chapter of First Corinthians teaches a cessation of the dramatic gifts when the Bible is completed involves far too many human assumptions to be accepted dogmatically. Certainly there is a vague possibility that it could be valid. From some standpoints the history of the church would seem to support it.

However, the Bible simply does not state this as a fact. Actually there is no Scripture that would prove a termination of the dramatic gifts at any time during the existence of the church on earth. It does teach very definitely that love is one of the graces that will endure long after many other things have passed away.

PART FOUR
The Message of the Church: the Gospel

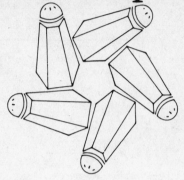

CHAPTER FIFTEEN
FROM SECONDARY
MESSAGES
TO THE GOSPEL

The earlier sections of this book would not be possible
without the gospel. By definition *revival* concerns
those who have already accepted the Good News. The
dramatic gifts are found only in the lives of those who
have heard the gospel and responded to it. *Love* is
impossible unless God's truth had indeed been the
"power of God unto salvation" in their lives. The
gospel then is fundamental. It has top priority and all
of the other fantastic experiences, gifts, and fruits that
the Bible describes must always remain secondary to it.

In view of the fact that all the other topics we
have discussed are either the results of the Spirit—as in
revival—or the gifts of the Spirit—as in tongues—or
the fruit of the Spirit—as in love—I think there
could be no better approach to the gospel than the
testimony of the Apostle Paul, who talked more about
the Holy Spirit than any other Bible author.

The third chapter of Philippians is a sort of doctrinal
life story of the apostle. In the first eleven verses
he details his religion and human goodness before he
met Christ on the Damascus Road, and then he
contrasts that with the changes that took place in his
life after his conversion.

After all we have discussed about revival, tongues,
and love, which are exciting subjects and mountaintop
experiences, it is a bit sobering to notice that Paul
follows his doctrinal exposition of his conversion
by talking about the Christian race and road—not

anything especially dramatic (verses 12-21).

Christianity is not always "exciting." Sometimes it is very routine. In fact, if we examine the work of the church realistically, we see several facets that are not particularly glamorous:

(1) Most of God's work is carried on by pastors and people of small and medium-sized churches. It would be difficult for any very large church to accomplish more than the accumulative hard work of the many small churches in any given area. This does not mean that any pastor should strive toward small numbers, little buildings, and few programs. But it is a fact that most good churches may never be large. However, this does not mean that they are ineffective. There are many things that can be accomplished by a small church that are impossible for those of us who pastor great conglomerates.

This is particularly true in the area of person-to-person contact between pastor and people. Personally, I regret this and do all I can to remedy it, but I am only kidding myself if I think I really know all of my people. In addition to this, small churches may be the only ones that will ever reach those people who cringe at the thought of being one worshiper lost among several thousand others.

On the other hand, some large churches are necessary. There are things that numbers and the resulting finances can do for a community that a small church could never do, particularly in the area of music, television, special guests, and the inspiration that a crowd engenders.

A small church may not add a very impressive figure to the statistic book. But put all the small churches together and they would make the results of the big churches look a bit sick.

(2) Most of the money given to the Lord's work does not come in large amounts. Only a fool would not be grateful for big donations. But the big total financially comes from a host of givers who are not wealthy. In 1976 The Peoples Church promised more than a million dollars for world missions—from one church. A breakdown of these promises would indicate a little more than 2,500 givers—children included. Only five or six would amount to ten or twelve thousand dollars, twenty-five or thirty would be between five and ten thousand, forty or fifty would range between two and three thousand, and the rest would be less than two thousand. As a matter of fact, by far the majority would be less than a thousand. Financially, God's big work is supported for the most part by God's little people. They don't have much but are generous with what they have.

(3) Most of our Christian lives are not lived on the Mount of Transfiguration, in the midst of dramatic experiences, or with a constant "turned on" feeling. Thank God, all of these are possible and everybody experiences them from time to time. But the day in and day out walk with God is fraught with tribulation, trial, suffering, disappointment, failure, and sheer hard work—praying when we feel there is no God there, reading the Bible when it does not appeal to us as the most exciting book in the world, and living for God on many days when we do not feel very much like a Christian. In this spiritual race, the crowd sometimes does not cheer very enthusiastically, and we must plod along the road with its many uphill climbs, and the weather is nasty. Sometimes even the scenery isn't very attractive.

The point is that God is with us during the sometimes heartbreaking laps of the racecourse, and

the Holy Spirit is still dwelling in us to empower
us for the sometimes monotonous and forbidding
stretches. We need to remember that Christianity is not
a permanent "ball," nor is it a "turn on" that is
a substitute for drugs or alcohol. It is a cross and a cross
is not pleasant. Furthermore, the path of the cross
is mostly uphill.

CHAPTER SIXTEEN
THE APOSTLE AND HIS RELIGION

The third chapter of Philippians, as we have already noted, is probably the best life story of the Apostle Paul that we can find anywhere in the Bible. Nearly the whole passage is based on his personal experiences.

In verses two and three of this life story we find a keen analysis of the essential differences between the religious man and the regenerated man: "Beware of dogs, beware of evil workers, beware of the concision. For we are the circumcision, which worship God in the spirit, and rejoice in Christ Jesus, and have no confidence in the flesh."

Verse two is a description of a religious man—the kind of man the Apostle Paul was before his experience on the Damascus Road. Verse three is a description of a regenerated man—the kind of man Paul became after his experience on the Damascus Road. Verse two is not only a warning to young Christians to beware of the Judaizers, or false religious teachers, but it is a picture of what the apostle was himself at one time.

Paul describes the religious man with three phrases—dogs, evil workers, and concision. He describes the regenerated man with three other terms—in Christ, no confidence in the flesh, and circumcision. In Christ as opposed to dogs. No confidence in the flesh as opposed to evil workers. Circumcision as opposed to concision.

LOST AND SAVED
As a religious man Paul was lost; as a regenerated man he was saved.

He describes the religious people of his day as "dogs," and of course Paul had been one of them himself. The word "dog" was used by the Jews as a term of contempt for the Gentiles. Jewish people in Paul's day, and most Jewish people today, were very particular about their food. Certain foods, according to law, are clean, while others are unclean. Some foods can be eaten by the Jew, but some cannot. When we see the word *kosher* written on the front of certain shops, it simply means that the food so described is ceremonially clean.

In the eyes of orthodox Jews, the Gentile people of the world have never been particular about their eating habits. They eat any kind of meat in any form or combination, seemingly without any discrimination whatsoever. When the Jew looked at the Gentile, and observed the fact that from the standpoint of Jewish dietary rules he ate both clean and unclean food, he immediately classed him with the dogs of the day.

Dogs then were scavengers. There was no such thing as canned dog food or chlorophyll dog biscuits. The dogs simply ate from the garbage heaps or from the leftovers and waste of their masters' tables. When the woman from the coasts of Tyre and Sidon asked Jesus for help, she reminded him of the proverb about dogs (outsiders) eating the crumbs which fell from their masters' table (Matthew 15:27).

As a result of this similarity between the Gentile and the dog, as far as eating habits were concerned the Jew began to call anyone who lived outside of Judaism a dog.

Theologically, in the New Testament the term "dog" was adapted and applied to anyone who was outside of Christ—not a believer. The book of Revelation, in speaking about the holy city, describes the people who

will not be there with this old Jewish expression: "for
without (outside heaven) are dogs" (Revelation 22:15).
Thus the word "dog" for the Jew referred to anybody
outside of Judaism, and the word "dog" for the early
Christians referred to anyone outside of Christ.

When Paul warns the Philippians to beware of mere
religion, he refers to the religious people of his day as
dogs. "Beware of dogs," avoid the person who is
religious but who is outside of Christ, or lost. The
Apostle Paul was numbered among that group at one
time himself. He was religious but he was not a child
of God.

In contrast, Paul describes the regenerated person as
being "in Christ."

Regenerated people are "in Christ" in the sense that
they are in the family of the Lord: "But as many
as received him, to them gave he power to become the
sons of God, even to them that believe on his name"
(John 1:12).

Regenerated people are in Christ in the sense that
they are in communion with the Lord: "Behold, I
stand at the door, and knock: if any man hear my voice,
and open the door, I will come in to him, and will
sup with him, and he with me" (Revelation 3:20).

Regenerated people are in Christ in the sense that
they are in love with the Lord: "We love him, because
he first loved us" (1 John 4:19).

Finally, regenerated people are in Christ in the sense
of that mystical union which can only be partially
described in such terms as branches in the living vine,
stones forming a part of a living building, and members
of a living body.

WORKS AND GRACE
As a religious man, Paul depended on his works for

salvation; as a regenerated man, he had no confidence in the flesh.

Paul describes the religious people of his day as "workers," but sadly, "evil workers." This again is what the Apostle Paul had been himself before his regeneration. No one could refute his claim of having been an ardent follower of the religion he believed in. He had been so desperately zealous in his attempts to oppose the work of the early Christian church, all in the name of religion, that he had "made havoc" of it.

The regenerated person goes about preaching the gospel and sowing wheat. The religious person works ardently preaching another gospel and sowing tares in the same field. That is exactly what these people were doing in Paul's day. He was sowing the wheat; they were sowing the tares. He was working, and they were working; but his work was building the kingdom of God, and theirs was attempting to destroy the kingdom of God. They were working, but they were working toward an evil end.

Possibly the greatest enemy of the early Christian church was to be found in the efforts of the Judaizers to move the young Christians from the simplicity of their faith in Jesus Christ back to the form, ceremony, and ritual of religion. From that day to this, the powers of darkness have been attempting to do the very same thing. If the devil can succeed in robbing Christians of their childlike faith in Jesus Christ, and can cause them to rely upon the form and ceremony of mere religion, then he will have accomplished his purpose.

The Reformation was necessary in Luther's day because the church had lost its belief in salvation by faith alone and had become a huge, cold, lifeless religious body. When Luther protested, he protested against this loss of simplicity; and when the Reformers moved out, they moved back to the biblical doctrine of salvation by grace through faith.

The spiritual and moral reformation which took place under the ministry of John Wesley was necessary because the Church of England had begun to stress its form and ceremony and ritual to such an extent that simple faith in Jesus Christ and holiness of life had become obscured. Although he never actually left the Church of England, he was often forced to preach outside of it in order to emphasize these truths once again.

When the Puritans came to America in the seventeenth century, they came for exactly the same reason—that they might be free from the ritual, form, and ceremony of the powerless church of their day, and so worship God scripturally and according to the dictates of their own hearts.

The great temptation of every new Christian group is to grow up and gain great ecclesiastical recognition. Usually this involves the building of a religious machine, the formation of an elaborate liturgy, and an overemphasis upon the scholastic standing of its clergy. All of these things, of course, have their place in the church. But history has proved many times over that with growth and maturity and the development of a machine, there is the danger of lack of power, dead formality, modernism, and worldliness.

Most of the regular denominations of our day were born in the midst of revival fires; but in a great many cases the devil has been successful to such an extent that the fire has been put out. When this takes place, the Spirit of God steps over the walls of these organizations and moves on to work among smaller groups who have remained faithful to the Word of God and have not allowed its simplicity to be obscured with man's machinery.

In contrast to religious people who are simply "evil workers," Paul speaks about regenerated people as having "no confidence in the flesh." The apostle was writing to a group of people who were proud of their racial origin. The same group in John the Baptist's day boasted to him, "We have Abraham to our father," whereupon he replied, "God is able of these stones to raise up children unto Abraham" (Matthew 3:9). They were proud of the fact that they were Jews. They not only boasted of their national heritage, but they were beginning to depend upon it for their salvation. John made it absolutely clear that the fact that these people were the children of Abraham was no credit to them. God could raise up children from the stones or dirt upon which they stood.

The Apostle Paul had a racial and religious background superior to that of the majority of the people to whom he was writing. Yet he was able to say, "I have no confidence in the flesh."

"Not by works of righteousness which we have done, but according to his mercy he saved us" (Titus 3:5). Christians know that no amount of praying, giving, working, or worshiping has resulted in their salvation. They have no confidence whatever in the ability of the flesh, but they have complete confidence in the efficacy of the finished work of Jesus Christ on Calvary's cross.

CONCISION AND CIRCUMCISION

As a religious man Paul practiced an empty formality; as a regenerated man he worshiped God in the spirit.

Paul refers to the religious people of his day as the "concision." Actually they were Jewish men who had in their bodies the mark of circumcision, a rite simply meaning that a man is set apart as a worshiper of God, he is in contact with God. The virtue of circumcision, however, is not the mark, but rather the reality for which the mark stands. The important thing is not the circumcision, but knowing and obeying God.

That is true in any sphere of life. The crown on the shoulder of a Canadian soldier does not make him a major. The crown is worn because he *is* a major. The important thing is not the crown—it is the commissioned rank for which the crown stands.

The religious people of Paul's day had the mark of circumcision, but they lacked the reality for which that mark stands; they had no vital contact with God. Therefore, Paul does not call them the circumcision, but "the concision."

"Concision" refers to a mutilation of the flesh which has no real significance. The bodily mutilations we have seen in pictures of some primitive tribes, among whom missionaries are working today, could only be called concisions, because they do not mean anything of eternal or spiritual importance.

If a Jewish man has no contact with God, his mark of circumcision is nothing more than a cutting of the flesh, or a concision.

In verse 3 Paul describes himself and other Christians as the real circumcision. Some of the early Christians were Jews, and had in their bodies the literal mark of circumcision. However, there were many of them that had come from the pagan world, and of course did not have that mark. But Paul describes all of them as the circumcision, because as believers they possessed the reality for which the symbol stands.

They were in vital contact with God. They were true worshipers of God through Jesus Christ; and so Paul says, "We are the circumcision, which worship God in the spirit."

The great danger of the Christian religion is to emphasize the symbols of our faith to such an extent that we lose sight of the reality for which they stand. Beautiful church buildings are designed to carry our eyes heavenward and thus make it easier for us to worship God, but it is quite possible to become so enthralled with their beauty that we lose sight of God. Then, of course, the symbol becomes meaningless. The cross is another symbol that has done a great deal to draw the attention of the child of God to the sacrifice of his Savior, but it is very easy to so emphasize the cross as a symbol of religion that we forget the Lord Jesus Christ and our obligation to him. The ordinances of communion and baptism and dedication become meaningless in themselves unless we are in personal contact with the Lord.

The essential virtue of the Christian religion is not to be found in its symbols but in its Savior; and when the symbols or the marks become the important thing and we lose the reality for which they stand, then they are nothing more than mutilations and we are little more than the concision.

People who are merely religious are lost. They are evil workers. They belong to the concision. People who are regenerated are saved. They have no confidence in the flesh, and as such they belong to the real circumcision. In our witnessing and soul-winning, our first objective must be to put people into contact with the living God through faith in the crucified and risen Savior, Jesus Christ.

CHAPTER SEVENTEEN
THE APOSTLE AND
HIS RIGHTEOUSNESS

There are many ideas that are incorporated in verses
four to eleven of the third chapter of Philippians,
but as a whole they present one major theme—Paul's
spiritual robe before and after he became a Christian.

"Though I might also have confidence in the flesh.
If any other man thinketh that he hath whereof
he might trust in the flesh, I more: Circumcised the
eighth day, of the stock of Israel, of the tribe of
Benjamin, a Hebrew of the Hebrews; as touching the
law, a Pharisee; concerning zeal, persecuting the
church; touching the righteousness which is in the
law, blameless.

"But what things were gain to me, those I counted
loss for Christ. Yea doubtless, and I count all things
but loss for the excellency of the knowledge of
Christ Jesus my Lord: for whom I have suffered the
loss of all things, and do count them but dung, that I
may win Christ, and be found in him, not having
mine own righteousness, which is of the law, but that
which is through the faith of Christ, the righteousness
which is of God by faith:

"That I may know him, and the power of his
resurrection, and the fellowship of his sufferings,
being made conformable unto his death; if by any
means I might attain unto the resurrection of the
dead."

If we were to think of verses seven and eight as the
pivot point of a balance, hanging on one side would
be verses four through six—describing Paul's goodness

as a man—and on the other side would be verses
nine through eleven, indicating Paul's godliness as a
Christian. Verses seven and eight—Paul's evaluation
of the two matters—are the pivot point of the balance.

As he considers what was his before he was
apprehended by Christ on the Damascus Road, Paul is
able to boast of a great deal more than the average
religious person of his day or any day. He lists seven
reasons for boasting—four which were his by
inheritance, and three by accomplishment.

INHERITANCE

His inheritance included four things that were greatly
admired in his day (verse 5).

Circumcision. The moment Paul said "circumcised
the eighth day," he elevated himself in the minds of
his Jewish readers above the heathen, the proselytes,
and the Ishmaelites. The heathen world had no
claim to the biblical ordinance of circumcision, and
therefore had none of the privileges of the covenant
that lay behind it. The proselytes were circumcised,
but always remained inferior because it was done
at the time of conversion. The Ishmaelites were also
circumcised, but not until the thirteenth year.
Thus the Jew who could say "circumcised the eighth
day" was considered spiritually superior.

Stock. The apostle then added that he was "of the
stock of Israel." Other nations had descended from
Abraham and Isaac and could claim the distinction of
circumcision, but only the Israelites had descended
from Jacob and could claim the promise of God's
covenant with Jacob. Jacob had wrestled all night until

God had blessed him in a singular way, changed his name to Israel, and declared him to be a prince with God. "Israel" was the highest title of God's ancient people. To use this name was indeed a privilege devoutly to be wished, and Paul had that privilege.

Tribe. Paul was further elevated in the Jewish mind when he said he was "of the tribe of Benjamin." This was important because it was from this tribe that Saul emerged as the first king of Israel. The tribe of Benjamin never wavered from its allegiance to the house of David, and it was in the territory of the tribe of Benjamin that the Holy City of Jerusalem was built.

Education. The fourth thing that was his by inheritance was a Hebrew education. He was able to say that he was "a Hebrew of the Hebrews," indicating that he was reared in a home which had maintained all of the Hebrew customs and probably spoke the Hebrew language. This was not true of all the Israelite homes; but there were in Paul's day a few families that were so utterly orthodox that they adhered to the oldest of Jewish customs and conversed with one another in the Hebrew tongue. Paul came from such a home. He was a real Hebrew.

ACCOMPLISHMENTS

The first four distinctions were his by inheritance. Now he mentions what was his by choice (verses 5, 6).

"As Touching the Law, a Pharisee." The Pharisees were the strictest religious sect of that day and everyone knew it! They were certainly closer to the kingdom than most of the other organizations of

that period. They were the most "spiritual" and the most orthodox. Sadly, their traditions and their religious pride kept many of them from Christ. A number of early converts to Christianity came from among the Pharisees. Nicodemus, that very zealous ruler of the Jews, was a Pharisee.

"Concerning Zeal, Persecuting the Church." Paul was not only a Pharisee, but a very active one. So zealous was he that he delighted in contending for his faith by persecuting the Christians because they constituted a threat to the whole pharisaical system.

"Touching the Righteousness Which Is in the Law, Blameless." According to the Jewish standard of righteousness, the Apostle Paul was able to say that he was irreproachable. He was ceremonially perfect because he had observed all of the ordinances. He was doctrinally perfect because he knew and believed the law. He was practically perfect because to the best of his ability, he had kept the law.

No wonder he was able to look the religious world of his day in the eye and say, "If any other man thinketh that he hath whereof he might trust in the flesh, I more."

Having said these things regarding his robe of human goodness, Paul then turns to a consideration of his robe of Christian godliness (verses 9-11).

"AND BE FOUND IN HIM"

To be a Christian means to be in Christ. As the branch is in the vine and draws its life from the vine, so the child of God is in Christ and draws life from Christ. If we are born again we are in him now, at the last day, and always.

To be in Christ means to be clothed in the righteousness of Christ—"not having mine own righteousness, which is of the law, but that which is through the faith of Christ, the righteousness which is of God by faith" (verse 9).

A few years ago I visited a sheep ranch in the hills of New Zealand. Near the homestead we noticed a small enclosure where there was one large ewe with a very small lamb—only a few days old. What caught my eye was the fact that the lamb was skipping about the pen wearing an "overcoat." Not only did he have his own fine covering of wool, but he had another complete lamb's skin over the top of his own. At first I thought he was just a Canadian lamb trying to keep warm in New Zealand. But then the rancher told me the story: Possibly his mother had given birth to triplets and then wandered off before the third baby was strong enough to follow, or perhaps the lamb had been orphaned in some other way. At any rate, he had lost his mother.

The ewe had lost her own lamb—perhaps he had died at birth—but she would have nothing to do with this strange-smelling orphan. The rancher had taken the skin from the ewe's dead baby and wrapped it around the motherless lamb, and the problem was solved. Now the bereaved mother smelled the coat of her own baby and began to take care of the orphan who was wearing it. The lost lamb had found a mother by virtue of the coat he was wearing.

There is probably no better illustration of what the Apostle Paul meant when he said, "And be found in him, not having mine own righteousness . . . but that which is through the faith of Christ." Christians find favor in the eyes of God because they are clothed in the righteousness of Jesus Christ.

How hopeless would be our condition before God if we had only the merits of our own righteousness to present! But how wonderful to realize that when we are "found in him" we are clothed in the spotless robe of his righteousness, and God looks upon us favorably because of Jesus. "He hath made us accepted in the beloved" (Ephesians 1:6).

"THAT I MAY KNOW HIM"

Not only does the Christian abide in Christ—as the branch in the vine—but we know him as a bride knows the bridegroom.

There are three ways that we may know a person. Sometimes we "know" a person who does not know us —that is, we know *about* him or her. Or, we may know someone by virtue of a formal introduction. When I am introduced to a man, I know him and he knows me. I know his name; he knows mine. I know his position in life, and he may know mine. Most of our acquaintances are this kind.

However, there are always one or two people in the world whom we know as we do not know others. Husbands and wives know each other in this way. They have loved one another and spent many years in intimate fellowship, and as a result really know each other. This knowledge involves feeling, sympathy, and understanding. This is the kind of friendship that stems, not from an introduction, but from a long period of close communion.

This is what is involved in the word the apostle uses here: "that I may *know* him." Not that I may read about him or be introduced to him, but that I may know him as an intimate Friend. This knowledge of the Lord is not the result of study, but of communion and fellowship. It is not so much a knowledge of the head as of the heart. The Christian who thus knows him can say:

And He walks with me, and He talks with me,
And He tells me I am His own,
And the joy we share as we tarry there,
None other has ever known.

For Paul, Christ was not only his life—he was in Christ—but also his Friend—he knew Christ.

"AND THE POWER OF HIS RESURRECTION"

The apostle had already experienced the resurrection power of the Lord on the Damascus Road, but he realized that this was only a sample of the power that would someday raise his body from the grave.

The same power that brought life back into the body which the Roman soldiers laid in Joseph's tomb has been experienced by every Christian. The resurrection power of the Lord Jesus Christ has worked within our hearts the miracle of the new birth. That power has brought us from death in our trespasses and sins to life in the Lord Jesus Christ. That power has transformed our lives from darkness to light. That power has made of us "new creatures" and caused old things to pass away, so all things might become new.

It is because we already know the resurrection power in our salvation that we can look forward with confidence and hope to the future glorious resurrection of our bodies.

"AND THE FELLOWSHIP OF HIS SUFFERINGS"

What a thought! The believer has the privilege of sharing in the sufferings of the Savior.

We can fellowship in the external sufferings of our Lord. He lived a sinless life, and as a result he was hated, rejected, and persecuted by the world, even before he went to the cross. As we live a holy life for God, we too will suffer the slings and arrows of a world that hates righteousness; but even while people revile us and persecute us and say all manner of evil against us falsely, we can remember that it is for his sake. And as we bear it, we fellowship with him in his sufferings.

We can also fellowship in his internal sufferings. He knew no sin, but in his humanity he waged a continual war against the temptations of the world, the flesh, and the devil. He "was tempted in all points like as we are, yet without sin" (Hebrews 4:15). What a consolation in the midst of Satan's onslaughts to know that we are sharing in the same kind of battle which Jesus fought before us. We have fellowship with him in his sufferings.

Finally, in a minor degree, we can have a sympathetic fellowship with him in his sufferings on the cross. No human being can ever share the burden that he bore or feel the pain that he felt or know the heartache that he knew. We can only look at the cup which he drained to the dregs. We can only stand on the edge of the storm through which he passed. We can only begin to imagine the abyss which he probed to the depths.

But as we contemplate his death on the cross, we can sympathize to some extent and thus know the fellowship of his sufferings.

"BEING MADE CONFORMABLE UNTO HIS DEATH"

Perhaps the apostle is looking forward to his own
death, and because of his relationship to the cross
of Christ he is prepared for it or conformed to it. More
likely he is talking about the crucifixion of the flesh
to which he had become conformed. He had reckoned
himself dead unto self and sin, that he might live unto
Christ and righteousness. He amplified this truth
in Galatians when he said: "I am crucified with Christ:
nevertheless I live; yet not I, but Christ liveth in
me" (2:20). We conform to the death of our Lord
insofar as we die to ourselves. Christ lives his life
through us.

"ATTAIN UNTO THE RESURRECTION OF THE DEAD"

"If by any means" does not express doubt but
humility. Paul considered himself the "chief" of
sinners, and for him to realize that he would have a
share in the final resurrection of the righteous seemed
almost too good to be true. The sheer glory of the
truth humbled him.

"I might attain" brings in the thought of arriving at
the end of a journey. Paul always thought of the
Christian as a pilgrim in a foreign land, traveling
toward home. There are trials and tribulations along
the way, but if we are "found in him," there is
resurrection and glory at the end of the road.

Paul had already experienced resurrection power in
his regeneration, and he anticipated the same power
in his body which would one day make him victorious
over death and the grave. For the Christian, the
heavenly life begins here and now. The life of faith is
the beginning of the life of glory. Both consist of
union with Christ. They differ only in degree, not in

kind. The life of faith, with all the hindrances of the world and the flesh removed, climaxes in the life of glory.

EVALUATION

On one side of the balance is Paul's robe as a man— his inheritance and his accomplishments. On the other side is his robe as a Christian. In verses seven and eight we have Paul's own evaluation.

In the light of the glory of his possessions in Christ, his inheritance and accomplishments began to shrink in his estimation until all that was left on the balance was a heap of "dung." Opposite the robe of his human goodness he wrote the words "no profit." "Yea doubtless, and I count all things but loss."

Then as he contemplates the glory and the blessings and the privileges that were his when he was clothed in the robe of Christian godliness, he could think and write only one word, "excellency." The Christian may have "suffered loss," but the profit is greater than the loss because Christ has been gained.

This is the gospel and it takes priority over every other doctrine or blessing in the Bible. There can be no fruit of the Spirit and no gift of the Spirit until we are temples of the Spirit as a result of hearing and accepting the gospel.

CHAPTER EIGHTEEN
THE APOSTLE
AND HIS RACE

Whether you have actually competed in a "miracle mile" or simply run in a "three-legged race" against your neighbor in a Sunday school picnic, you are familiar with the terminology of the racecourse. The people to whom Paul was speaking were familiar with the sport of racing, and when he used this illustration of the Christian life in the third chapter of Philippians, they knew exactly what he was talking about. This is one of several passages in the New Testament that draw an analogy between the Christian life and some sort of athletic competition.

"Not as though I had already attained, either were already perfect: but I follow after, if that I may apprehend that for which also I am apprehended of Christ Jesus. Brethren, I count not myself to have apprehended: but this one thing I do, forgetting those things which are behind, and reaching forth unto those things which are before, I press toward the mark for the prize of the high calling of God in Christ Jesus. Let us therefore, as many as be perfect, be thus minded: and if in any thing ye be otherwise minded, God shall reveal even this unto you" (verses 12-15).

If we are to be successful in any kind of race, whether it be against flesh and blood on one of the racecourses of this world or against principalities and powers on the spiritual racecourse, certain attitudes are essential.

DISSASTISFACTION

Dissatisfaction is the first step toward spiritual progress. Paul says, "Brethren, I haven't arrived; 'I count not myself to have apprehended' " (verse 13).

He was not unhappy with his physical or material state of prosperity. He was one man who had learned in whatsoever state he found himself, physically or materially, therewith to be content. In this letter to the Philippians he makes it clear that he had learned how to abound and he had learned how to be abased. He could get along with a great deal or he could get along with very little (4:11, 12). But he was hungry for moral and spiritual progress.

The springboard of advancement, even on the level of everyday life, is dissatisfaction. There is no progress without it. It was only because someone tired of living in a cave that today we live in houses. Because people became dissatisfied with being clothed in the skins of animals, we find ourselves clothed as we are today. If the world had never wanted something more than a horse and buggy could provide, we would not be driving automobiles and riding trains and buses. Because women didn't enjoy doing the wash with a scrub board, today we have automatic washing machines. Dissatisfaction is the first step toward progress on any level.

In the spiritual world, the principle is the same. If there is no dissatisfaction spiritually, there will never be any progress spiritually. It is absolutely essential that there burn within the breasts of all Christians a thorough-going discontent with their present moral and spiritual life.

The important thing is not the victories we have already won, but the victories that still need to be won—not the ground we have already gained, but the great area that still lies within the hand and the power of the enemy. If we dwell upon the blessings we have already received, there will be no incentive to reach out for the multitude of blessings still to be claimed. If we stop after we have gone the first mile, we will never go the second mile. If we relax after we have won one soul, we will never win a score of souls. If we are content when our church is supporting five or six missionaries, we will never attempt to support more. We must focus our attention upon what still needs to be accomplished. This is essential.

Perhaps the greatest blight upon many of our Christian churches and Christian people is the fact that we have gone a little way, we have accomplished something, we have gained ground, we have won a few victories—and we have become satisfied. We have stopped. We are marking time, and in many cases we are stagnating. Pollution and corruption result.

OBLITERATION

The apostle says that we must not only be dissatisfied with the present, but we must obliterate the past— "forgetting those things which are behind" (verse 13).

There is a sense in which memory of past sins can keep us in a position of humility before God, but there is another very real sense in which memory of the sins of the past can become a brooding that impedes our future progress. Repentance of sin is one thing. Repining over sin is another. If our sins are confessed, they are forgiven, they are cleansed. If they are cleansed, they are to be remembered against us no more, forever. If God forgets, how much more should you and I forget. It is possible to so dwell upon past failures that our possibilities of service and blessing in the present and the future are destroyed. Growth is then impossible.

There are some Christians who base their hopes for the future on the statistics of the past. They failed last year—therefore, they will fail next year. They have always lived a defeated Christian life—therefore, they always will live a defeated Christian life. In the past, they have gone down under the pressure of temptation—therefore, in the future they will succumb to temptation. What they have been, they will be. They are basing their expectations for the future on the statistics of the past.

This kind of Christian needs to remember that the power of God can change the course of the statistics. God can transform failure into success, weakness into strength. Defeat can become victory. For the Christian, the future does not depend upon the past. It depends upon the power of God.

Where would some of the great characters of the Bible have been if they had been content to base their hopes for the future on past performance? The third chapter of the book of Jonah commences this way: "And the word of the Lord came unto Jonah the second time . . ." This was after Jonah's experience with the great fish. If Jonah had been like a great many modern Christian people, as he stood on the shores of the sea with his experience of defeat and failure behind him and God gave him a second opportunity, he would have said, "It's no use. I was called once, and I did not respond. I received a commission to preach at Nineveh, and I turned my back and found a ship going to Tarshish. Find somebody else to fulfill the commission. I am a failure. I always have been a failure—therefore, I always will be a failure."

If Jonah had done that, perhaps over 600,000 people

in the city of Nineveh would never have received God's message, but Jonah was able to forget the things which were behind. He was willing to obliterate the failures of the past and move on toward the city of Nineveh to preach in response to the call of God, with the past behind him.

We all know the result. The Spirit of God fell upon Jonah and transformed his failure into success and his defeat into victory. The city of Nineveh heard God's message and was spared.

Perhaps the most brokenhearted man in the world at the time of the crucifixion was the Apostle Peter. There he stood in the midst of a worldly crowd, warming his hands over the world's fire and denying that he had ever been associated with his Lord. He was defeated, discouraged, broken.

Approximately fifty days later, on the Day of Pentecost, the Spirit of the Lord came upon the same man and told him to stand up and preach. Peter might well have said, "Find someone else to do the preaching. I can still remember that day in the upper room when I professed that I would lay down my life for the Lord Jesus if necessary, and yet before the cock crowed the next morning I had denied him three times. I cannot preach—I am a failure. I cannot answer the call of God any longer. I cannot rise to a position of leadership, because my actions in the past have proved that I am weak and incapable of assuming such a responsibility."

Peter might have talked in this manner, but he did not. He was willing to forget the past, and the power of God fell upon him in such a way that when he stood to preach that day 3,000 men and women responded. Once again God had changed the course of the statistics. God used a man who refused to base his hopes for the future on the stumblings of the past.

"Forgetting those things which are behind" involves obliteration of the sorrows of the past as well. I have known some Christians who dwelt so deeply on the sorrows of the past that they destroyed the possibility of joy and usefulness in the future. Bereavement has crossed their path, disappointment has found its way into their lives, or sickness and disease have handicapped them, and for years they have been nursing a broken heart. They have refused to be comforted. They have turned their backs on happiness. They have avoided blessing, and as a result they have been useless to themselves, to other people, and to God. They have never put aside the sorrows of the past. If the Christian really believes in the reality of the resurrection, how foolish it is to weep forever at the grave.

The attainments of the past must go too! The Christian is not meant to glory in a previous golden age, but upon the golden age which is yet to come. The limitless possibilities of the future should be the standard—not the achievements of the past. We should always remember that no matter how much we may have received already, the best is yet to come. For the Christian the best wine is always reserved for the last. The future is the most glorious.

CONCENTRATION

It is not enough to be dissatisfied with the present and to obliterate the past. We can do both of these, and yet stand still on the Christian racecourse. The third word must characterize our lives if we are to be successful in reaching the mark. There must be concentration.

Paul says, "This one thing I do" (verse 13). He was
a success because he was a "one track man." He lived
for only one thing: that he might be a witness to
the saving power and grace of God. That is all!
Everything else was secondary. He had a singleness of
purpose, a concentration of life, energy, and ability.

Analyze the career of any eminently successful man
and you will discover that whether he be a businessman or a professional man, the focal point of his
entire life is his work, and everything else is wrapped
around it. Everything else is secondary. He lives,
eats, breathes, laughs, plays, sleeps, and dreams his
work. The reason most people do not succeed is that
they try to do too many things. A man is only able to
concentrate upon one thing. If he does, he succeeds.
If he does not, he fails.

The Christian needs to realize that he has been left
in the world for only one purpose—that he might
be a witness to the saving grace of God. That is why
the Christian is a father second, a professional person
second, a mother second, an employee second, a
golfer second, a homemaker second, everything else
second—and a witness first. Christians are in the
world to be witnesses, and they must concentrate on
fulfilling their calling.

Paul describes the extent of his concentration by
the words "reaching forth" (verse 13). When a runner
is racing at full speed, toward the end of the course
his "second wind" usually puts him into overdrive
in an attempt to overtake his competitors. To do this,
he has to use all of his reserve energy and power.
He stretches his body out to its full extent, holds
nothing in reserve, giving the race everything he has.

This is the idea that Paul is putting across when he
uses the words "reaching forth." He is thinking

of the racer using that last little bit of reserved energy and power in order to reach the mark. The reason most of us do not run as well as we might is that we hold too much in reserve. Some of us have talent which has never been dedicated to the Lord. We have energy which has never been made available to God's work. We have brainpower that has concentrated on other things. We have time which has been spent on the world. Many of us have never really stretched out for God. We have never given God everything. We have never exerted that last little bit of energy. We have never called up the reserve.

Paul says that if we are to run well for God, we must concentrate upon giving God our very best: "This one thing I do . . . reaching forth unto those things which are before . . ."

THE MARK AND THE PRIZE

The Christian is running toward the mark, not the prize. The mark, in an ordinary race, is the line of white ribbon at the end of the course, indicating the finish of the race. The concentration of the runner is never upon the prize, but always on the mark. In the Christian race, the mark is not happiness, but holiness. It is not paradise, but perfection. "Be ye holy, for I am holy." The children of God are aiming at that holiness of life and character which will be a constant witness to the world in which they live of the saving power and grace of God.

We concentrate upon reaching the mark, but it is clear that someday we are to receive the prize. The prize is not given out on the racecourse—the prize is to be given out at the Judge's stand. And if we have run well, there will be a time when we will hear the

voice of God calling us higher. In response to the
"high calling of God," we will move from the
racecourse of life up to the Judge's stand, where we
will receive the prize.

We concentrate on perfect holiness, and we are
rewarded by perfect blessedness. We strive toward
moral and spiritual perfection, and we are rewarded
by eternal paradise. We reach out to gain the mark, and
someday we are called higher to receive the prize.

If we are regenerated, we are on the spiritual
racecourse. If we would run well for God, our lives
must be characterized by dissatisfaction, obliteration,
and concentration. "Brethren, I count not myself
to have apprehended"—dissatisfaction. "Forgetting
those things which are behind"—obliteration. "This
one thing I do"—concentration. The mark is holiness
and the prize is heaven.

This may be the least dramatic outcome of our
salvation, because it involves the everyday effort of
being conformed into the image of God's Son. There
may be a few dramatic and exciting experiences along
the racecourse, but most of it involves spiritually
putting one foot down after the other until the "mark"
is reached, and that takes a lifetime—maybe a few
years, maybe seventy plus. Only then has the Holy
Spirit finished his work. Then we are ready for the
"high calling."

CHAPTER NINETEEN
THE APOSTLE
AND HIS ROAD

The Apostle Paul urged the Christians of Philippi to use him, and other people like him, as an example for their Christian lives.

"Nevertheless, whereto we have already attained, let us walk by the same rule, let us mind the same thing. Brethren, be followers together of me, and mark them which walk so as ye have us for an ensample. For many walk, of whom I have told you often, and now tell you even weeping, that they are the enemies of the cross of Christ: Whose end is destruction, whose God is their belly, and whose glory is in their shame, who mind earthly things. For our conversation is in heaven; from whence also we look for the Saviour, the Lord Jesus Christ: Who shall change our vile body, that it may be fashioned like unto his glorious body, according to the working whereby he is able even to subdue all things unto himself" (3:16-21).

On May 13, 1940, Sir Winston Churchill made his first address to the British House of Commons as Prime Minister. In that speech he said, "I have nothing to offer but blood, toil, tears, and sweat." These words were heralded around the world in the headlines of our newspapers as among the great original statements of our generation. Undoubtedly this was an important thing to say, and the world felt its effect to the full; but most people who are interested in literature realize that John Donne said almost the same thing in the year 1611, and Lord Byron repeated it in 1823. Churchill knew when to say it again, and how to adapt it to the crisis at hand; but even Sir Winston Churchill was not absolutely original.

Most of our learning comes as a result of imitating other people. The psychologist calls the people we imitate "models," because in a sense we model our lives after theirs.

This is just as true spiritually as it is physically. Christians imitate other Christians, and a great deal of what we learn spiritually comes from watching others and patterning our lives after theirs. Of course, we realize that the supreme example of all Christian living is the Lord Jesus Christ himself. Despite this fact, the Apostle Paul recognizes that most Christians will look for help to other people, and to some extent arrive at a pattern for their Christian living from them. These verses indicate two kinds of models whom we could imitate, the sinner and the saint.

There are five differences between these two, and Paul describes them vividly.

ALLEGIANCE

The basic distinction between the sinner and the saint is that one owes allegiance to Christ, the other to the world. The sinner is described as belonging to a group of people who are "enemies of the cross of Christ." Saints are citizens of heaven, "for our conversation (citizenship) is in heaven."

People who take a stand in opposition to the cross take their stand with Satan. They are opposed to the work of Christ, they recognize no obligation to him, and they are not on their way to heaven. They owe their allegiance to the archenemy of the cross, the devil. In contrast, saints have knelt at the foot of the cross, have accepted Jesus Christ as their own personal Savior, and their names have been written down in the Lamb's Book of Life. They owe their allegiance to Christ.

OBJECTIVE

The objective of the sinner is to gratify the flesh— "whose God is their belly." The objective of the saint is to crucify the flesh. Paul refers to his body as "vile."

The sinner lives to satisfy himself, to fulfill his own ambitions, to cater to his own desires. Appetite is his master.

Although the Apostle Paul would be the first to proclaim the fact that his body was "fearfully and wonderfully made" and the temple of the Holy Ghost, he also recognized that the materials of the body are dust and ashes. It is the body that is subject to the diseases and infirmities and sinful desires which limit the capacity of people to such an extent in this life. In one sense, it is the body that drags them down and away from God. With these thoughts in mind, Paul condemned his body as vile; and in many instances throughout the epistles he talks of crucifying the body, or putting it down in order that he may better live for God.

All the endeavors of sinners are concentrated upon their objective in life—to gratify the flesh. All of the efforts of the saints are concentrated upon their great objective—to crucify the flesh, and as a result let the Lord Jesus Christ live through them.

SENSE OF VALUES

Saints weep over their sins; sinners glory in their sins. When Paul describes the life of worldly people, he is so wrought up about their sin that he says, "I now tell you even weeping..." As a Christian, sin is so horrible to him, so destructive, that the very thought of it breaks his heart. Now he describes another kind of people, those who revel in their sin, "whose glory is in their shame." The very thing over which one weeps, the other glories in. What makes one ashamed makes the other proud. What one hates, the other loves.

Sin has so perverted and warped the minds of people that they actually boast of things of which they should be thoroughly ashamed. They rejoice over those things about which they should weep. But godly people are ever conscious of what sin did—it caused Christ to die on the cross. Of what it is doing—it is creating the corruption present in the world today, ruining homes, and blighting lives. Of what it will do—it leads to destruction. This, of course, makes the saints hate sin, and even the thought of sin almost crushes them.

INTEREST

The concern of sinners is this world; the concern of saints is the next world. Sinners not only live in this world, they are attached to it. Their roots are in it, and they are a part of it. They "mind earthly things." They are living in this world, and for this world. Their attention is focused on the business and pleasure of the world.

The saints are living in the world, but their hope lies beyond it. They "look for the Saviour." They are in the world, but not tied to it. They are on the world, but not rooted in it. They do their task here, but their home is over there.

The same oceangoing vessel can carry immigrants leaving their homeland and citizens returning to their homeland. The first group will weep when they say farewell; the second group will rejoice. Immigrants leave behind them all that is dear to them. Their roots and their family are in the old world. Everything for which they have ever lived is there. When they set foot on a ship, they sail into the unknown, leaving everything behind. On the other hand, returning citizens have no such love for the country they have been visiting. Their family is not there. Their friends are not there. Their business is not there. They do not really belong there. They can rejoice because they are setting foot on a vessel that will take them to the world to which they belong. They are going home.

That is what makes the difference between the saint and the sinner when it is time to die. Each one of us must someday board the ship of death. At such a time sinners are fearful and they weep, because they are forced to pull up roots in the only world with which they are familiar and head out into the unknown. Whereas we saints set foot on the ship of death with confidence and hope, and sometimes even rejoicing, because in a very real sense we are going home. We are headed for the land of which we are citizens. Sinners shudder at death because they are interested in this world. Saints meet death with a steadfast hope because their interest is in the next world.

DESTINATION

Finally, Paul makes it clear that there is a difference of destination. The terminal for the sinner is judgment—"whose end is destruction." The terminal for the saint is resurrection—"that it may be fashioned like unto his glorious body." Sinners live their lives with their allegiance to Satan, their objective to gratify the flesh, their sense of values to glory in their shame, their interest to mind earthly things, and their destination to be destroyed. The saints owe their allegiance to God. Their objective is to crucify the flesh. Their sense of values is to hate sin. Their interest is in the next world. And their destination is resurrection.

Jesus said exactly the same thing: "Enter ye in at the strait gate: for wide is the gate, and broad is the way, that leadeth to destruction, and many there be which go in thereat: Because strait is the gate, and narrow is the way, which leadeth into life, and few there be that find it" (Matthew 7:13, 14).

CONCLUSION

As Christians, we must follow and model our lives after someone. We may choose to follow the sinner whom Paul has described in detail, or we may choose to follow the saint with whom Paul has associated himself. May God grant that we will make the right choice.

This decision is vitally important, not only because of its effect on us, but also because of its influence on others. We will follow someone and someone will follow us.

Are you the kind of mother a daughter can follow? Would you want your son to go in his father's footsteps? Would you feel justified in saying to your Sunday school class, "Make me your example"?

The Apostle Paul seems to be saying that religion is not enough—regeneration is necessary. That there will be a "Damascus Road" experience when our inadequate righteousness shrivels up into a pile of dung and we are wrapped up in the righteousness of Jesus. That after we have been born again, we find ourselves on the racecourse of life, trudging toward the mark. But that the race may be a sort of super marathon mostly involving walking, plodding from day to day—often out of sight of the grandstand—until we finally find ourselves, by the grace of God, back in the arena surrounded by a great crowd of witnesses and ready to receive our crown. "Well done, thou good and faithful servant: thou hast been faithful over a few things, I will make thee ruler over many things: enter thou into the joy of thy Lord" (Matthew 25:21).

EPILOGUE

The problem with writing a book of any kind is that there is really no good place to stop. Perhaps that is why so many stories in "the olden days" ended with the words "and they lived happily ever after"—which is another way of saying that we could go on talking about these events but we must stop sometime.

This is particularly true of any writing, preaching, or teaching about the Christian faith. You can never say it all, and no one can include every topic that deserves attention. Many years ago Dr. J. Wilbur Smith was my guest in The Peoples Church for a Bible conference. He had just finished his fine work about heaven and promised he would send me a copy. I was surprised when he told me that there had not been any *definitive* book written on the topic—certainly not in modern times.

I remembered his use of the word "definitive" because I don't think I had ever heard it used in this way. I looked it up in the dictionary and learned that among other things it means, "serving to decide something; conclusive." When I read Dr. Smith's book, it certainly came very close to giving an exhaustive resumé of what others had taught about heaven, and of course a scholarly exposition of what the Bible says about the subject. However, it was not definitive, in the sense that for me the book never really concluded; it opened new windows, pointed to unexplored galaxies, and expanded vistas of thought that can be definitive only in eternity.

Therefore, without finishing this book, let me put in a period and say "the end"—even though it isn't.